stylinaut

Brad Baumgartner

SPUYTEN DUYVIL

New York City

Excerpts of this manuscript have appeared in *The Operating System* (Ex Spec Po), *Coffin Bell Journal*, *X Ray Literary Magazine*, and *Tarpaulin Sky Magazine*. Additionally, *Stylinaut* was shortlisted for the 2019 Tarpaulin Sky Book Award.

ISBN 978-1-956005-00-4
Cover Image: Danylo Movchan, *Saint*, 2018

Library of Congress Cataloging-in-Publication Data

Names: Baumgartner, Brad, author.
Title: Stylinaut / Brad Baumgartner.
Description: New York City : Spuyten Duyvil, [2021] |
Identifiers: LCCN 2021032713 | ISBN 9781956005004 (paperback)
Subjects: LCGFT: Poetry. | Prose poems. | Experimental fiction.
Classification: LCC PS3602.A965 S89 2021 | DDC 818/.609--dc23
LC record available at https://lccn.loc.gov/2021032713

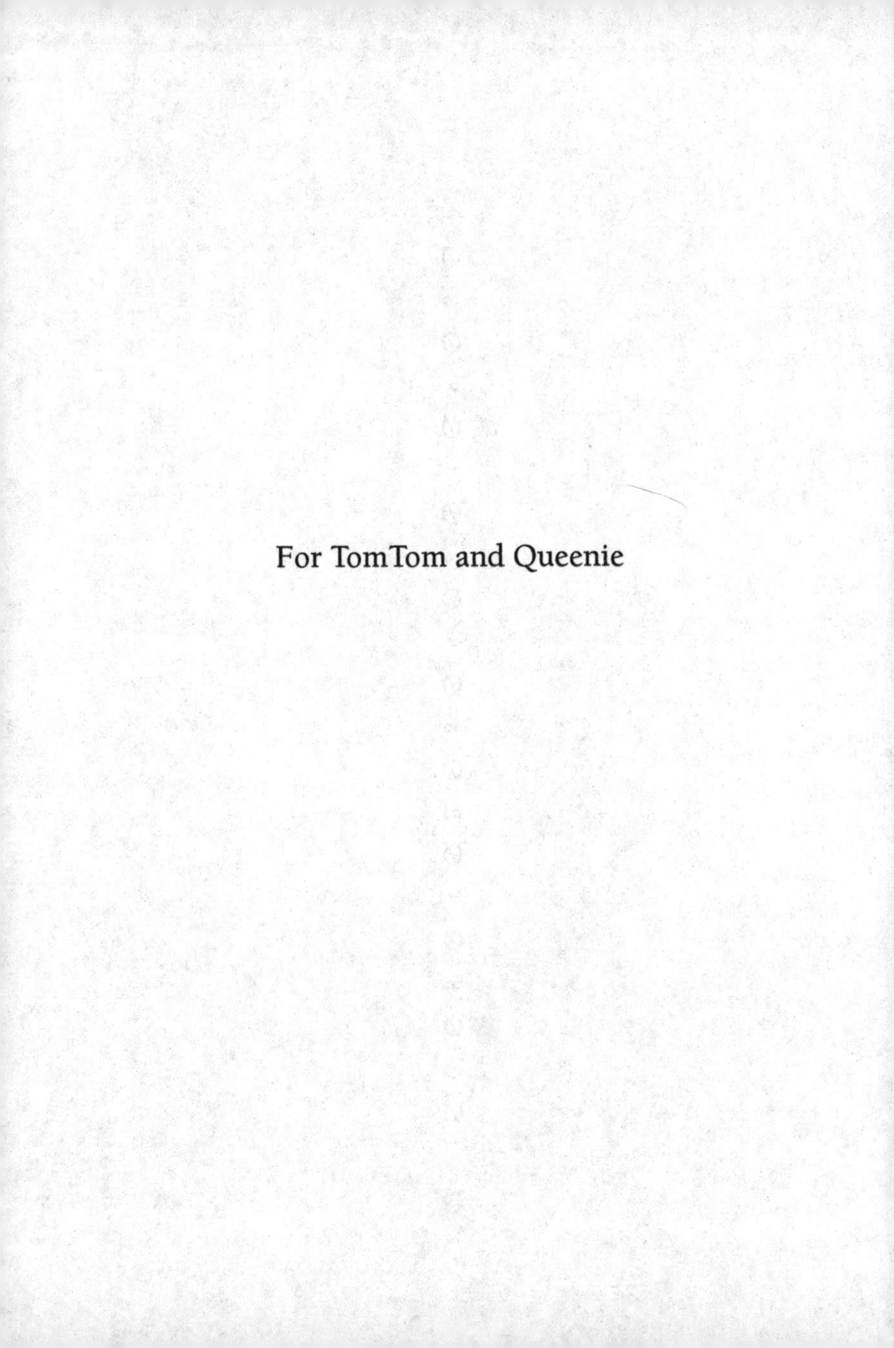

For TomTom and Queenie

Ø

∞

Ø

∞

Ø

∞

Ø

∞

Ø

∞

Ø

∞

Ø

∞

Ø

∞

Ø

∞

Ø

∞

Ø

Contents

"Writing is utter solitude,
the descent into the cold abyss of oneself."
—Franz Kafka

"To remain in solitude is a natural sign springing from the hearts—of non-attachment and the like."
—Milarepa

"We must assume our existence as broadly as we in any way can; everything, even the unheard-of, must be possible in it. That is at bottom the only courage that is demanded of us: to have courage for the most strange, the most singular and the most inexplicable that we may encounter."
—Rainer Maria Rilke

“Therefore start first with yourself, and resign yourself. In truth, unless you flee first from yourself, then wherever you flee to, you will find obstacles and restlessness no matter where it is.”

—Meister Eckhart

“The work is the death mask of its conception.”

—Walter Benjamin

Prologue:
Catacombs And Honey

To Vanquish is to Vanish

The desert saints took unprecedented risks. They often spent years in isolated retreat secretly practicing self-transforming physical and mental exercises. Some ascetic saints, known as stylites, took to the perilous task of ascending columns in order to live on small platforms atop tall pillars.

Housing the musings of Gregory Fremont Balder, or "Fremont the Stylite" as he affectionately became known among his frequent visitors in the desert, this peculiar book traces the (a)cosmic and styli-anagogic explorations of an astronaut turned modern day desert ascetic who turns to living atop a pillar in order to deepen his ascetic—physical, mental, meditative—and writing practices in order to do perform *fana* or ego death. Through a series of seven chapters, Fremont the Stylite (1965-2009), also known to his contemporaries as Mission Specialist Pseudo-Isambardo of Toporas, traces his soulside journey of anarcho-mystical auto-erosion.

The 'Stylinaut', a portmanteau of a modern-day astronaut turned stylite (or ascetic "pillar dwelling" saint), vigorously climbs up the tiers of his desert pillar, with the ascent ultimately putting him at seventy-seven feet above the ground. Committing himself to writing, the stylinaut moves through the double desert of himself/world and world/cosmos. This action manifests from a burning desire to be rid of desire, an aporetic sensibility that renders him completely in-sensible, but also curates his body and mind for divine union. Hence, each new stop on the pillar (there are seven pillars total, each eleven feet in height) sees the stylinaut parsing through the spiritual ordeal of his facticity, one characterized by the deeply sorrowful yet ecstatic experience of embodiment. By way of a series of short poems, fragments, and philosophical aphorisms, he is lead and un-leadened through a masterful maze of self/world naughting, rendering inside-out as Outside-in.

The figure of the stylinaut is a metaphysical triplet,[1] an acosmic drifter who partakes in the solitary diurnal gesture of trying, as Meister Eckhart might put it, "to

1 Referred to in three ways throughout the book—Charles Freemont Balder, Freemont the Stylite, and Mission Specialist Pseudo-Isambardo of Toporas—it is safe to say that there are anonymous, pseudonymous, and pseudepigraphical, albeit Trinitarian, traces in these writings.

forget [himself] and everyone" by traversing the abyss of himself. His mission is simple: to forget, he must remember; by remembering, he must forget. Always already remembering and forgetting, he sojourns the trials and tribulations of life via a mode of detachment made of equal parts joyous and acerbic. Turning inside out and outside in, he nearly vanishes into thin air, being-playing his ludic lute into the resolutely Absolute. Yet it is facticity alone which allows him to find his way home, floating like a buoy into the mist/midst of the impossible, and for this he is simultaneously resentful and humbled by his very own existence—that exuberant retrograde honor-horror which slithers like a set of honeyed marbles in and out of his own hands.

The practice of writing as a kind of forgetting (i.e., awakening via intense self-investigation; becoming by dis-remembering; being qua self-subtracting) de-creates a mode of thought wherein to vanish also means to vanquish oneself. Here we find an experimental collection of aphorisms, fragments, dialogues, and poems which hovers between a work of speculative fiction and a non-philosophical treatise, that is, between theory-fiction and fictional theory. Self-contradictory and self-subverting, completely incomplete, often evidenced in its sometimes-abrupt shifts in focus from the divinely stupefying to the horrors of self and world, the book remains doubly non-sensical. In one way, it does not take itself too seriously simply by knowing that sometimes it takes itself much too seriously. In another way, this non-sense also points to the senselessness of the losing one's senses via ecstasy or, alternatively, having found them lost or displaced due to bewilderment. Who is Mission Specialist Pseudo-Isambardo of Toporas? Well, he is simply someone who becomes what he is, and could easily be both you and I; and *neither* you, I, nor of any of us at all, that is, no one.

There is, of course, no such Pseudo-Isambardo of Toporas. After all, he eventually writes himself to the very cusp of blissful nothingness and, one might say, loses himself completely—perhaps to find himself elsewhere one day: moving between being and non-being, consciously. As a writerly ascetic moving in and out of pseudonymous impersonality, he is both speaker and deaf mute, the spoken and the silenced. There is also *only* Pseudo-Isambardo of Toporas, that is, he is everything because he is no one. (To vanish is to vanquish as to vanquish is to vanish.) As he float-walks through meontological Space, we can attribute to his pseudonymous authorship the quadru(bi)p(ed)al meaning of Isambard (derived from the Old German name Isanbert and means "glittering iron") and bardo (in Tibetan Buddhism, it means a state of existence between death and rebirth), and "toporas," which is both a flower (Violet) and in Romanian translates into "bury the hatchet."

A Secret Power

Keeping in mind Nietzsche's peak to peak formulation,[2] the tradition of the aphorism can be said to run parallel to the joyous cry of the pinch, the jolt, of a courageous redistribution of consciousness from what happens *over there* to what happens spontaneously Now. Aphorisms and fragments thus hold a secret power, an anagogic seed of instantaneous pineal re-awareness and psycho-geo[holo]graphical redistribution. As a heuristic, the

2 In *Thus Spoke Zarathustra*, Nietzsche writes: "Whoever writes in blood and aphorisms does not want to be read but to be learned by heart. In the mountains the shortest way is from peak to peak: but for that one must have long legs. Aphorisms should be peaks—and those who are addressed, tall and lofty. The air thin and pure, danger near, and the spirit full of gay sarcasm: these go well together. I want to have goblins around me, for I am courageous. Courage that puts ghosts to flight creates goblins for itself: courage wants to laugh" (*The Portable Nietzsche*. Trans. Walter Kauffmann. New York: Penguin Books, 1954, 152).

aphorism compels these instantiations via the double modality of what we could call *whipped thought*. On the one hand, this is a direct allusion to whipping systematic thought against itself, as if tied to its own tree of knowledge, one wrongly rooted from the bottom and growing upwards. On the other hand, there is a colloquial expression of whipped (i.e., whipped cream) wherein thought itself is thrashed into a frenzied amorphousness, a preternatural ooze winding up its spherical serpent nature. This colloquial definition is perhaps indicative of the cosmic contingency of thought. The cosmos is the indexical handmaid of the human being; and yet, the human being becomes the vessel for an acosmic Mind's Eye. In this sense the aphorism holds a negative utility, warping habitual patterns of thought into a no-thingness where one might find oneself free of illusions, ties, worries. The aphorism issues an imperative. It stirs a reader to declare "no"; to walk away from the herd mind; to negate the often-ignominious fallacy of "who" one is in favor of finding oneself at the impossible edge of their own self-created abyss, wherein to live is to die, and to die is to live in the mega Ur-moment of perpetual bliss.

Yet to *find* oneself at the edge of this abyss is a paradox. How does one find oneself if one is trying to *lose* oneself? Is one not ultimately lost? Yes and no. This paradox is perhaps best described as the kōan of self-subversion, the playful yet daunting field of impossibility in which the mystic wanders through the world as a foreigner.[3] This meontological nomadism, in which one meanders up and down a path to nowhere, which is also to say, follows all paths everywhere, is a practical technique that can be used to undo the irreverent curse upon our pathetic fallacies of the self. Needless to say, "who" one is ultimately must be evacuated or destroyed. But how does one subvert the self when the very impetus which hyperstitionally brought them to such a point might continue to manifest the very desire of which one is trying to rid oneself? Perhaps the simple answer to this question is to do nothing at all, to remain detached at all costs, which costs nothing.

This aporia is indicative of Meister Eckhart's famous prayer to God to rid himself of God.[4] And so, at the limit

3 The self as foreignness is beautifully professed by Georges Bataille when he writes that "the essence of myself arises from this [...] the feeling of my fundamental improbability situates me in a world where I remain as though foreign to it, absolutely foreign" (*Inner Experience*. 1954. Trans. Leslie Anne Boldt. Albany: State University of New York Press, 1988, 69).

4 Cf. "Thus we say that man must be so poor that he is not and has no place wherein God could act. Where man still preserves some place in himself, he preserves distinction. This is why I pray to God to rid me of God, for my essential being is above God insofar as we comprehend God as the principle of creatures" (*Wandering Joy: Meister Eckhart's Mystical Philosophy*. Trans. Reiner Schürmann. Great Barrington: Lindisfarne Books, 2001, 214).

there is juncture; the impasse, a bridge. Pessimism and mysticism are two different sides of the same strange coin: a trodden, blackened coin, the worst coin which has buried itself underneath the treasure chest of "life," tricking the metaphysical pirates so as not to get taken with the other loot! Oddly enough, this negative worthless coin is a true token of spiritual wealth, a hidden treasure bound by the economy of the blur, as it enacts an auto-liminal exchange in which all is dwindled down to nothing and back into All. This auto-marginality is where the spirituo-epigrammatic wanderer walks—backwardly, picking up and hiding the breadcrumbs they once left behind in the forest so as never find oneself as *that* person ever again.

Le(a)v(en)tating:
Amid the Overman and the Non-Man

Against the all-too-typical affirmative logic professed by modern "self-help" culture or the naïve, often misguided, self-"seeking" norms of motivational speaking, these pessi-mystic aphorisms find eureka actualized in the des(s)ertion of self, a kenotic autophagy rendering sweet the baseness of self and world—and their corollary banes—in order to ferment or give rise to a negative dialectics of *self-rec(o)uperation*.

On this point, two figures come to mind that might help us to frame this observation: the Overman and the non-man. Nietzsche's concept of "the Overman" (Übermensch), a pinnacle figure in *Thus Spoke Zarathustra*, is a man willing to risk everything for the sake of humankind in order to overcome life's inherent meaninglessness. Unlike Nietzsche, E. M. Cioran did not believe in the possibility of an Overman. Rather, he searched for what he called a "non-man,"[5] a man "totally imbued with his nothingness." The stylinaut levitates between the two figures via a kind of auto-

---

5 Cf. "Cowards, we substitute the sentiment of *our* nothingness the sentiment of nothingness. It is because the general void disquiets us not one whit: in it we see all too often a promise, a fragmentary absence, an impasse opening up... For a long time I have searched for someone who would know everything about himself and about others, a demon-sage, divinely clairvoyant. Each time I believe I had found him, he obliged me, upon scrutiny, to sing a different tune [...] What a disappointment! And I [...] no longer dreaming of a non-man, a monster who might be totally imbued with his nothingness. It is madness to conceive of him: he could not exist, absolute lucidity being incompatible with the reality of the organs" (*The Temptation to Exist*. Trans. Richard Howard. Chicago: U of Chicago P, 1968, 191).

fermentation, that is, a *le(a)v(en)tation* of self-des(s) ertion. To undergo and to dwell in suffering is to secretly move in and through the edible darkness, creature-walking the marginal space between the Overman and the non-man, the mystic and the pessimist. But let us ask *you*, dear reader, are not those who have endeavored to evacuate themselves of their subjectivity the Overmen of New—which is really to say, when properly inverted to its coreless and shapeless infinity, the Dead of Olde?

Of the stylinaut, we ought to ask one more question: Why writing? Why not just hold it all `in, hold it at bay? On the one hand, writing may be completely useless, the symptom of a kind of delirious confusion with what one is writing about; the act of writing being nothing more than a pathetic aberration. On the other hand, perhaps it is a form of *heart-work*, the carotid-corollary to ethically enacting compassion (for the Other). To sever the cosmos from one's subjective "narrative of becoming" would be a blatant and ignominious disgrace, for "to be" we must simply become what we are, and it is trifling to subject oneself to a kind of causality which regards who one ought to be with what one really is. As such, a kind of ethical, rather than a merely ontological, conundrum subsists in this pseudo-narrative of becoming, as if one *cannot* know what is right for oneself at any given moment by way of their own inexistence. (Now, what the will can do that mere intention cannot—this is perhaps a deviation from the Tibetan Buddhist doctrine of compassion—is another story altogether.)

One must be careful not to confuse oneself with the one's writing, however, as to do so would be like confusing the ontic with the ontological. In a writing practice which emphasizes kenotic autophagy, there is no "out there" and "in here." Rather, the Outside inheres our insides. We are always already psycho-etherically eating ourselves, so to speak. As such, the stylinaut's space suit is an inside-out body which le(a)v(en)tates in the des(s)ert-Space between the Overman and the non-man, actualizing the speculative profundity—or pro(o)fun/d(u)ty—of his composite self-naughtings vis-à-vis his final mission of composing stylinautical missives.

The aphorisms and fragments contained herein are liminal nodes, unheard whispers in the cosmic desert of thought, which at certain times sit unmoving, anchoring the weight of the pessimist's reality of worst. At other times, these whispers are given voice. The anchors are set free, opened to whimsical wisps of wind which move like sandstorms, caking sand halos onto one's head in this very same desert. And yet, like all sand structures kissed by the wind it falls away again into its own auto-annihilating formlessness. These words thus meet at the juncture of anchor and sand, hell and heaven, non-movement and fleeting exemplarity. And in a hidden compartment within the hidden treasure chest, black diamonds, housed in the fluidic repository of a saint's unending nothingness and pressed underneath the impossible weight of pessimism's heaviest heaviness, are suddenly revealed.

According to this formulation, these pessimo-mystical aphorisms of inversion, ecstatic poems, and diamond-hardened fragments speculatively unveil the tropes of misguided non-living in order to sever the preconceived notions of the everyman, to cut ties with illusory ways of living that are losses of—and to—a truly spiritual life. The non-space existing among this triumvirate writerly nexus thus becomes the ungrounded ground for the weeding out of thought. It curates a mode of hyper-elucidation which elicits thought's coming up through the cracks and entails a breaking up of the systemically laid concretism of one's own compulsive projections and projective identifications with the illusion of things, the world, and oneself. By coming up through these cracks, epigrammatic thought reveals the negative instantiations of who-one-is and *detracts* from them; this is where the manicule points at the cracks in oneself, where one pulls out their ego filters as weeds. From here, on this groundless charnel ground of systematicity, one can dig the tombs of who-one-was-once, an act of de-creation which meanders into a realm replete with nothing—nothing, that is, but the exclusive conditions for mystical rapture. Once one is *not-there*—where one is, to follow Pseudo-Dionysius the Areopogite, "neither oneself nor someone else,"[6]—then, and only then, will one grow back together, backwardly, which is also to say *rightly*, to walk upside-down through the world-mire, warping the axis of time and space via the invisible rose-cross of spontaneous and true self-love: that is, horizontally on one's hands and vertically with one's feet into the "third heaven,"[7] where neither the thought of nothing nor nothing itself exists, not even the third heaven.

The 'Four Purges'

A reading non-experience of this sort also engenders, through the a-musical angels' chorus of healing one's spiritual deafness, a corollary psycho-aural attunement

6 "*The Mystical Theology.*" *Pseudo-Dionysius: The Complete Works.* Trans. Colm Luibheid. New York: Paulist Press, 1987, 137.

7 Cf. 2 Cor. 12:2: "I knew a man in Christ above fourteen years ago, (whether in the body, I cannot tell; or whether out of the body, I cannot tell: God knoweth;), such an one caught up to the third heaven."

in which one pineally unlistens to a cacophony of subverted selves, each voicing itself in the last instance from an impossible throat at the spontaneo-saintly non-moment of thought's severance: the dawning of a halo. The shadow deflected from the glow of this halo thus makes the invisible visible, auto-bookmarking the secret pages of pessimo-mystical bibliomancy via the ears of a listener who hears-without-hearing and the eyes of a reader who sees-without-seeing.

This inherently playful collection, if it is to be taken seriously at all, thus seeks nothing—at all—but to foster spontaneous nodes of heresy uttered from the unspeaking mouths of one's self-subverted projections, opening to a readerly horror and corollary Joy which are offered in similar fashion as the liminal movement of the mystic's alternating experience of dukkhic suffering and its corollary nirvanic bliss. These musings are attempts to stand very, very still. Each text object (fragment, aphorism, poem) is a remnant or node of the stay, words written while sitting in the lotus position of obscurity, the pure etchings of a fourfold purge[8]:

8 Etymologically speaking, purge stems from Old Latin purigare, from purus "pure" + root of agere "to set in motion, drive; to do, perform" (from PIE root *ag- "to drive, draw out or forth, move").

purgative

[purgatorial]

[[purg(or)atorical]]

[[[purg-oracular]]]

The four purges unite in the deactualization of self and world, a purifying decrustification (of the world) and disintegration vis-à-vis the intrinsic quaddripp(l)ing (of melted selves), to unveil-unite in a succession of esoteric truths.

While held still the stylinaut begins to move, dancing as a peripatetic skeleton with nothing but wind in the body. The excess waste of oneself is expelled (moves) not through the anus, but by snakily moving up the spinal column via the various chakras. In between the vertebrae subsists the oft-horrifying ambiguity of spiritual ascent. These pessimally carved-out spaces are begotten of an ancient place before these "selves" ever existed—long before and ever-after one yanked oneself from Spirit and placed oneself in the womb. Only by sitting very still may one heal their broken back, a complete acceptance of weakness wherein one finds the strength of True Will to eventually stand upright and move *through* oneself. Midway through his upward journey, in "Opus Gregorius," he stops to speak to the crowd below him.

Ultimately, the great mystery is beyond the grasp of intellect. It cannot be seen or spoken. But what can be "voiced" [9] in part is the movement through the passage.

As Magmus of Indigo, stylite predecessor to Pseudo-Isambardo of Toporas, wrote in *The Lost Book of Acumens*:

To simultaneously hold
and let go of the hatchet—
To be buried and to bury.

The hatchet is you…

To forgive is to forget.
To be buried is to bloom.

Let us, then, follow Psuedo-Isambardo of Toporas as he embarks upon his *stylinau(gh)tical* journey of spirituo-meontological nomadism.

In this collection, the Dead of Olde are recast as the

9 In *Language and Death*, Giorgio Agamben posits that "the Voice … says nothing; it does not mean or want to say any significant proposition. Rather, it indicates and means the pure taking place of language, and it is, as such, a purely *logical* dimension. But what is at stake in this will, such that it is able to disclose the man the marvel of being and the terror of nothingness? The Voice ... wills *that language exist*, it wills *the originary event* that contains the possibility of every event" (*Language and Death: The Place of Negativity*. 1982. Trans. Karen E. Pinkus and Michael Hardt. Minneapolis: U of Minnesota P, 1991, 86-7).

Mystics of New, wiping their tears off the inverted lapel of the reader's second coming. This Corpus Christi-without-us is what ought to be, the anarchic redaction of oneself at the limits of mystical de-semblance, and what really *is*—which is also to say, what *is not*—as one smolders oneself in the negative resin of aletheia, where both angels and devils come out to play together in an effort to bury the hatchet.

Tripoietic Forgetting

Gleamingly rendered from the burning sensations of a darkened, lyrical quietude, this experimental book ultimately takes as its focus the limit-experience of an interfaced poetic practice, that is, it opens speculatively to the nonsensical via the triple conjunction of poetic performance (experimental writing/spoken word or oration), hyper-sensuous mixed meta-awareness (synesthetic auto-bewilderment), and mystical utterance (what Denys Turner terms the "self-subverting utterance"[10]). Symptomatic of a writerly state of aural conjunct-ivitis, the book encodes seven separate but

10 "[T]he utterance which first says something and then, in the same image, unsays it" (*The Darkness of God: Negativity in Christian Mysticism*. Cambridge: Cambridge UP, 1998, 21).

related sections consisting of meditative fragments, poems, and philosophical aphorisms: each unresponsively corresponding to an overarching apophatic mode of what we might call *tripoietic forgetting*.

This praxis of forgetting secretly indexes a kind of loopy thinking or a conveyance that reduces meaning to its superlative (musical) form and enhances writing to its least meaning-full (most playful) form. As the product of a speculative and unequi*vocal* mis-understanding, this book can be thought of as a bewildered auto-commentary, one that tiptoes up to the po(i)etic edge of radical negation and jumps off, performing the very synesthetic liminality of the divine unintelligibility it once sought to understand.

At the soundless dawn of the stylinau(gh)tical speculator's life-in-death, wandering alone and unbound, bound together as One, Fremont the Stylite's writings will se(a)mingly coalesce in ecstatic fits of tripoietic forgetting. And in the night sweats of this fever dream of utter darkness called Life, all one really can do is silently listen to seeing's silence: and what one hears, the utter(ed) and *only* Thing heard, is the barking white silence of the word's immanent auto-displacement vis-à-vis thought—that is, *a writing*.

…and this writing grows the flower of the Light.

In the desert
I saw a creature, naked, bestial,
Who, squatting upon the ground,
Held his heart in his hands,
And ate of it.
I said, “Is it good, friend?”
“It is bitter—bitter,” he answered;

“But I like it
“Because it is bitter,
“And because it is my heart.”
—Stephen Crane

Part One: Daring Desert

(The Writings
Of
Freemont The Stylite)

PILLAR I: HERESY

| |

(Zero Gravity Minus "Me" Equals Seven)

: : : : : : :

Wide-open sandscapes swallowing my tongue.

Daring desert;
courage of solitude.

Audens Solitudo.

: : : : : : :

Amorous again, and dealing without cards.

Yours unruly.

You know what you think about it,
and it will take you at your word for it.

So much for me…

: : : : : : :

Breathing from the vantage of a detaching cosmos.

Detaching from the cosmic vantage of breathing.

Assuming the position of cosmic detachment.

The cosmic non-breathing of disadvantage.

:::::::

Incorrigible blots on onanistic continuums.

Endlessly caressing the leaven of nothingness.

:::::::

Songs of meon (μή ὄν).

:::::::

Stop hiding behind the waitlessness.

:::::::

Handed microgravitational waving.

:::::::

Underneath the weightless.

: : : : : : : :

Sophistmatriculation.

: : : : : : : :

Chthonic Waving of a Hand.—Fed through the mouth of a vortex, life crushes. And yet, the strife of your netherworld comes hardly by way of mere distanciations. Rather, there it is, right there: the way out or the way in, hovering as joy just on the other side of your palm as you glide your hand through a wind.

: : : : : : : :

Mopping up oneself, and rid of the Illusion.

: : : : : : : :

To Diurnally Annihilate.—The metaphysical vomit that proceeds from diurnal annihilation is but the glistening morass of one's melted ego filters, fraught only with beginning an elusive chase (…into the abyss). Preparing for annihilation is, like any good father would a wayward son, to await *in toto*.

: : : : : : :

A Collective Deformation.—There is no community in lemming-being. They live to live another day, while they ought to rid themselves of "life," to become One with that which, erased, is both here and beyond.

: : : : : : :

A perennial stomachache.

Sick are those who negate the proposition of a looming, universal negation.

: : : : : : :

Rapture.—It is hardly an infraction for a newly beloved to be asked to wait forever in darkness. Ceasing, scattered drops of rolling water halt on the table of Love. Towards the nomenclature of eternality rolls the tongue of the One's formlessness. "Onward to the shadow throne," they excitedly murmur. Squirming, wriggled, a soft laughter ensues.

: : : : : : : :

Degenerate Nobodies.—They obsess themselves over things that, when siphoned, curdle spines. Spineless, they argue for themselves that they are themselves. Endless worlds of mirrors block the images of their possession. Possessed, they are petals in the grasses of the de-ranged. With lightning speed, many massive doubts thus implore the throes of masses of ignorant smiles.

: : : : : : : :

On Deception.—A two-faced man has only one face if, and only if, his crooked smile is seen by Janus during an impromptu head-shaking. At any other time, a double intemperance keeps truthfulness at bay: the artificial joy at holding one's tongue and a rigorous cathecting of goodwill towards null people.

: : : : : : : :

I am condemned to be "me."

: : : : : : :

Forget Yourself.—When it's all about you, it's hardly about anything else. In fact, what else could there be when it's all about anything at all?

: : : : : : :

A Most Important Question.—When asked, "When is your date of birth?" one might do better not to reply with a day of the year, but rather with the recitation of seven events that can be said to have taken place due strictly as a result of your birth. If mere six or less statements ensue, rephrase the question as such: "Do you mean the last time I was coy enough to dodge the absolute ineffability of my own existence?"

: : : : : : :

Regimen.—If everything you need will be given to you, then is it not strange that you possess quite a contrite little life? Why on earth would you inflict such ineffective rhetorical cruelties onto your own individual narrative? Why would you refer your affirmation to an outside party, as if the echo of your own dissolvable self-image is not the bane of your very existence? These sorts of questions, if asked of oneself in severe and unadulterated doses, become the breakfast of champions.

:::::::

Thought's puppeteers.

Pestering thought-puppets.

:::::::

Unthought Of.—What is thought's non-correlational foreground? Do we think or are we thought?—Do we penetrate thought or does though penetrate us? Or neither; or at all?

:::::::

A Capacious Horror.—"Thank you for your face," murmurs thought. To will emphases on expressions or facial curvatures is about as effective as putting the wrong emphasis on the wrong syllable. There is no modeling thought. Thought immanently and simultaneously evokes the cosmic negation of what is human: affective soirees, muscular comportments—mere *sapientisms*—are egoistic at best. Uses of the brows may signify deviations and perversions in thought. Eyes moving wistfully about or glazing over are merely fluctuations in the intensity of beholding. Leave excavations of facts and non-facts to the lie detectives. Often one's face appears inhuman.

: : : : : : : :

The tomb wench of the death of thought.

: : : : : : : :

The Taoist and the Ascetic.—Blankness is bliss. Fasting is feasting. The Taoist and the ascetic are not blood brothers, but rather empty crucibles, inverted vessels in which all that is earth must lay barren. To achieve a world not according to us, thought must sever one of two hands. To achieve a world not according to world, this severed hand must fasten itself to itself. Untying the fastened hand of Being with its only hand is like thought overcoming the difference between the Taoist and the ascetic. Simultaneously, with only one hand, the former must be let go of while the latter is held onto.

: : : : : : :

On the Wrong Foot.—What on earth is the reason for all of these thrashings about? Do you not tire of waltzing in clown shoes? Have you not tripped over one thousand times? And now what, you wear binding shoes underneath your clown shoes? It is all so limitless that you put limits on it, to keep from spitting vomit. It is all so limitless, and yet you wear binding shoes underneath your clown shoes and thrash about.

: : : : : : :

Mystified at Their Forgetfulness.—"Forever and a day" has become a colloquial expression completely devoid of the ubiquitous bliss of its true actuality. In its cultural reception, the expression is actually the impulse of a failed potentiality for collective anamnesis. The horror! To have forgotten of divinity's immanence is the insidious default mechanism imparted to modern society's children.

: : : : : : :

Remaining silent.

Mainlining silence.
Silently remaining.

::::::::

Sil(a)ncing.

::::::::

Most "conversation" is just miscommunication via oblivious auto-commiseration. (Just *who* do you think you're talking to?)

::::::::

Before a word is spoken, there ought to be at least seven soundless internal testaments given for its credence.

::::::::

Observing the categorically mutilating corrugations the deformed collective projects onto infinity.

To know that there is absolutely nothing better said than nothing at all.

: : : : : : :

Choosing one's words carefully,
as if one's very birth depended on it.

: : : : : : :

Dining Out.—It serves one well to corral in full measure with freaks, crusties, drifters, yogis, mystics. Drink a cup of coffee with a Green Beret. Pucker your lips for the walking wounded. Let the werewolves rip your veins out. The frigid cold will always eat your toes. But only few eat at the table of a wizard.

On Not Saying Too Much at Dinner.—If one manages to corral in full measure with the brethren of nil, always keep at least three secrets. Be a sponge, but do not be a sheet of glass. One must protect one's aura.

: : : : : : :

The train hopping stench of the profane.

The scantily-clad scent of ontological nakedness.

Imbibing the olfactory intensity of the unknown, the sacred, the communal.

: : : : : : :

Catatonia is like Blight in Spring.—One will always have those hands, that nose. What is corporeal is what most believe to be material. But true tremors of mind will leave even the hardest of harlots crawling at the feet of the Christ. Thus, when the jowls become numb do not try to swallow. Instead, take the time to inhale with fervor the tenderness of your lover's kiss, as they bend down gently to take back the life you stole from them.

: : : : : : :

Under Breath.—Words are often whispered when one wishes to share in a simpler, more intimate mode of communication, whether with oneself or with another. There is a brightness and a lightness to the sound of the whispered voice. It enacts a sense of play wherein one re-conducts the forgotten symphonies of childhood— *à la* willed shortnesses of breath. Whispers: auto-melodic asphyxiation.

Between Breaths.—A mighty crevice hollows the intensity of a gentle whisper's truly monolithic negative implications. Just atop the mountain, where all the echoes fall, plays the dirge for mindful breath.

: : : : : : :

The Highest Form of Love.—Whistling is an orchestration of self-love. Self-love, not to be confused with that lampoon called self-authorship, is a high form of love. If one cannot love oneself enough to let go of oneself, then by what stretch of the imagination could one have a capacity to even nod at a stranger without giving away the duplicitous dexterity of their knotted self-image? One does not have to (and should perhaps not) like oneself to effectively love oneself.

: : : : : : :

The Anxiety of Intellection.—When in the morning the brigands of non-knowledge come to steal your thunder, sigh in relief. They would not come for you if you were not entering new zones. In pillaging, they will validate you in ways that even your shrewdest friends cannot.

: : : : : : : :

To attend the lecture of a dead philosopher, a philosopher who has truly learned how to "die before they die."

: : : : : : : :

Sitting in the lecture hall of non-being.

: : : : : : : :

Seeing vis-à-vis the hearing of furtive glances looking right at you—this sight as the gnomic, aural site of non-being-toward-birth.

: : : : : : : :

Professor Hemlock.

: : : : : : : :

In the corner of the lecture hall of Being, a wily student named Sophia perks up when she hears Professor Hemlock's discussion of anxiety:

"We are here today to discuss your rattling heart. In Heideggerian terms, anxiety is that which discloses to Dasein its finality— death is what lies closest to us, structuring being through the death of being. In my unknowable estimation, his existential secret dwells outside of subjectivity insofar as it is unknowable as an object of thought; withheld from the subject because of an ontological instability: one, for instance, in which the Lacanian analysand might actualize the Real via a willed reconciliation of the symbolic and the imaginary. However, alienation can be apprehended only upon its own bearing out, as a concept borne out of being itself, for itself, via feelings and emotions. And because any talk of anxiety must take place within a language discourse, *anxiety-as-concept* will remain markedly different from the *anxiety-as-feeling*. It is anxiety as the process or product of feeling that interests us most, and that language must now try to comprehend, more or less syllogistically. Dialectical in design, any "passionate struggle *into* being," as the novelist D. H. Lawrence once put it, implies a passionate struggle *out of* being, a post facto Catch-22 of the ego-state. To say 'I' implies the resolution of the Lacanian impossibility: the death of the 'ideal-ego' in favor of the birth of the 'ego-ideal'.

But, dear students, there is tension, worry, wasted

personal energy, in any discussion of anxiety-as-feeling as it relates to subjectivity: occluded within its own autonomy, anxiety is the emblem of its own manifestation. Hence anxiety is indexical. As indexical, anxiety refers back to itself; is the manifestation of anxiety via its own encoded ontological structure—the object of anxiety as mediated by one's subjectivity, not as mutually competitive but as demonstrative."

Hearing the seeing of Professor Hemlock's lecture,

Sophia blinks about,
nearly blanked out
(and unabashedly so!).

Professor Hemlock continues:

"Let us try to understand it this way. To borrow from a Derridean formulation, there is not anxiety and non-anxiety there are *anxieties*, which are more or less comprehensive. Derrida once famously remarked that "there is not narcissism and non-narcissism, but narcissisms which are more or less comprehensive." My substitution of "anxiety" for "narcissism" in this case is merely a rhetorical choice, but anxiety is never wholly freed from its disjointed referent, however, because it serves as a spectral interlocutor, that is, a place marker residing both everywhere and nowhere. Phenomenologist Dylan Trigg once asserted that "*Anxiety is narcissism and narcissism is anxiety*." Here, in this formulation, we might say that the substitution comes full circle because it is already tied up in its own playful language game, and we may use the words interchangeably; although it is inherently relativistic, the substitution is not whimsical. Refusing to speculate on the duplicitous dichotomy of anxiety (ontologically, as a feeling, versus linguistically, as a term), the substitution, semantically culpable, inscribes its own otherness with receptivity while attempting to reconcile the dichotomy via comprehensiveness. The "more or less comprehensive" anxieties are narcissistic insofar as they are comprehensive and, contingently, they are comprehensive insofar as they are narcissistic. This is the strange contingency of a theory of substitution: it is not theory *of* substitution, but rather theory *as* substitution, an actualized self-referentiality. Hence this theory of substitution is already tied up in a theory of anxiety that corresponds to a more ontological register, theory *as* anxiety. We can thus make the following statement: *Theorizing is anxiety and anxiety is narcissism and narcissism is anxiety*."

On her way out of the lecture hall, Sophia almost passes out.

Sophia must learn how to die before she literally dies.

:::::::

A Slippery Slope.—Betrayal unwinds one's convalescence, whereas acceptance admits one to sit for a night on the pillowed throne of non-desire.

:::::::

The Magnet of Contingency.—There were always one thousand thousand paths to take in any direction at any given time. Contingent on each path taken and each non-path were not only these paths and non-paths, but the possibility of each path's and non-path's electro-pneumatic opposite.

:::::::

Opening to the inevitable magnetism of cosmic delirium.

Never again remiss.

: : : : : : : :

On Sluggishness.—The anguished and lethargic movement of emotional availability in the face of the sour-faced horror of realizing one's life is only as manageable as the degree to which one has done away with the impropriety of expectation.

: : : : : : : :

Tell Me, Who are You?—The imbecilic fallacy of a photographic memory; the inverted smirk of a dead end path.

: : : : : : : :

Schopenhauer's Song.—The curmudgeon plays the gutted fiddle of lurching.

: : : : : : : :

"I'm a Space Person."—The astronaut, Story Musgrave,

whose paradoxical views on knowledge and enlightenment, especially on the point of cosmic darkness, which becomes for him a mode of negativity in which one must become 'not' in order to become everything, is none other than a space mystic.

:::::::

Honorably Discharged.—To relieve oneself of the duty of being someone.

:::::::

Nothing is everything only after I am gotten rid of.

Not holding up in the cosmic court of law.

Withholding any evidence of myself.

:::::::

Cryptozoological Walks.—Walking underneath the water, my foot dips into the air. If I fall into the world, I will surely be suffocated by their habitual breathing techniques as they hack up hairballs of ignorance, torturing the animals housed within. It has been said that we know more about space than we do about the depths of the ocean. This is factual on the level of the sociology of knowledge formation. But what does an undine care about divisions between above and below? One must walk underneath water before one can walk on water. It must be implored: drench yourself via cryptozoological walks of the non-human.

: : : : : : :

In the Shadowlands.—The shadows of conflicted human natures, sitting in the town Square, are juxtaposed against the sordid Bay of Vasculitis. And when the honorable judge beckoned their call, they all sat and stared. A man stated that he had been eaten by a mountain goat. Another woman stated that she was a descendant of Zhang Jue. A little shadow of a nymph with a muffin top said that she wouldn't go anywhere without her lawyer. Just then, three men in white shirts and gray pants came upon the crowd, threw black paint on them, and yelled, "Ye be He, the Ones, the Three! We shall slay you down!" Upon watching the scene, the honorable judge turned to an old man beside him, a man, in fact, that knew what he was going to say because he had seen this all happen some forty years before in a dream—and the judge said, pointing over there, "You are all free to go. But before you do, don't forget to lift those horses out of their cages. Their legs do not work any longer." The old man turned to the judge with his keen old set of eyes, ones that lay barren and full of silk within his decrepit body, and replied, "You, sir, are the King of Ages, and have bid us welcome into the Throne of Ambiguity. At last! We shall no longer be still but are free to wander the Mountain of Infinite Granite." In two days' time, the group could not lift a single horse out of its cage. They died in the Square and the judge ate their hearts.

:::::::

A shielder to die on.

:::::::

All memories are post-spacetime spiral-traumas.

:::::::

redwoods house distressed elves
as the sylphs pet our heads

: : : : : : :

mellifluous sirens
drinking dexterous drinks….
upon their throats,
the utterance of a jinx

: : : : : : :

Beyond-Stretched.—The speculative horizontal space in which the mind-body split has been usurped and negated via its own endless stretching out of itself on the torture rack of Being. This strain is the coming face to face with the beautiful horror of being stretched horizontally back into infinity.

: : : : : : :

Post-Traumatic Stress.—The epiphanic conjunction of the sonic curvature of not-being-oneself via the immensity of inner space; affective remembrance via meontological convergence in the auto-incinerating chamber of somatic memory recall.

: : : : : : : :

To give oneself up.

: : : : : : : :

Reflecting nothing, undelivering, and not from this shell.

: : : : : : : :

De-creating, and dying with the creator of the birth of the end of life.

: : : : : : : :

Lost, always,
in the midst
of this mist.

: : : : : : : :

NOW: the no-where lilies grow and
the Sun of God bespeaks the Mysteries.

: : : : : : :

Stepping
beyond
belief.

PILLAR II: META(EK)STASIS

| |

(Bog-Bodied Hermeticism)

: : : : : : :

The Marshman Prophecies.

: : : : : : :

Bog day sunrise.

: : : : : : :

Mata / (Devi)
Stigma / (Bacterial Endocarditis)
Stigmata / (Bacteresy)

: : : : : : :

The musculo-skeletal convolution-volition of feeling what/one's remains.

: : : : : : :

Schizo-affective rain falling from the tear ducts of
eyes that cannot yet see and
ears that cannot yet hear
their own
f a l l i n g splendor.

: : : : : : :

tunneling sandworms—
temporary
and seekingly

: : : : : : :

Your Own Inter-Personal Wormhole.—The space-time con*undrum*tinuum of actualizing a tunnel between your own and another's fistula.

: : : : : : :

Dawn of the Black Hearts.—The sneaking suspicion that one is already very completely dead.

: : : : : : :

Gone Mad for the All.—Filthiness need not be conjoined to unreadiness. Many a mad hatter has seen ecstatic glimmers of radiant suns, all while dirty crown to toe. Madness is unearthly to the extent that its unkemptness is *a closeness to God.* Pathways of grime are engrafted to the body, forming sigils of individuation.

:::::::

This Body?—A question arises: What is it that propels the necessity of the body to be itself? To be unfailingly and relentlessly hurled into some sort of cosmic origin point, the body passing as an abyssic grave. Is it the body that gives way to the cosmic origin point? Or rather, is it the cosmic origin point that gives way to the body? Fingernails draw my drifting body back into itself as my hands implore the great cosmic wake of 'I AM'.

:::::::

A Higher Organ.—Accounting for the body becomes a sort of medi(t)ative conundrum in which the phenomenological experience of the body as body must be mediated through the ether, of a meditative non-experiences of the body. The body can be accessed only through the un-doing of itself.

The Commentary of the Divine.—The commentarial paradox of the body reads thus: if one must have a body, then the body is not only a commentary on the divine, but also the commentary of the divine. The body in itself is not of itself. The body is itself through a kind of autopoietic journalism, wherein the way one feels and what one is combine in the maddening, blackening, and liberating assemblage of somatic memory recall. When un-experienced, the body becomes the commentary of the divine.

: : : : : : :

feelings so
sharp
and edges as
knives
grow inklings
and as
worst inevitable

: : : : : : :

G r i e f:
Fissure-grower of the eternal,
a cosmic mourning working
itself out through
the bodymind;
NOW catalyzed

and the paradox of the flesh.

: : : : : : : :

Temple of the Mourning Scar.

: : : : : : : :

The unwinding woundology of the wound(il)logical.

: : : : :: : :

I am I(?): chthonic disjointedness; terrestrial bleeding; the phantom limb of spectral disembodiment.

: :: : :: : :

Cloak of Mausoleum.—Some see clothes, styles, attitudes. But to see only covered bodies—bodies that cannot be hidden, that are so close to death that the vultures hover above them. Decrepit, the dead body is immanent, always already destroying itself into deliriously morbid states of repulsion.

::::::::

Meontology of the entropic body/
the negentropy of my ontology.

::::::::

Uncompromised.—The Everything and the Nothing; a crystalline slime ballooning diamonds from a corpse.

::::::::

That Thing is Not the Body.—The arrival of something so completely foreign—again the flesh must take the brunt of bio-hauntological inundation. "To what end?" one might ask. And yet that seems to be the wrong question, as if our bodies were ever really ours to begin with. Whatever happens there, to that body, to a body, has been taking place for all time and will continue to do so.

::::::::

Rather than be the victim of suffering, accept the body's

indecision as Christ infinitely mounts the cross, for his body was not mounted on it, but was the cross itself. What was left over, the flesh of presence, was mounted on the cross.

::::::::

Not the body.
Not not *the body.*

::::::::

Corporeal castration.

::::::::

Aporia of ontic minutia,
I engrave an invisible collarbone for Thee.

::::::::

The smell of hospital breath: the inverted phantasmagorical dining out of the end of history.

:::::::

A Man and His Wound.—A laceration persisted on the man. It stretched from his navel all the way up to the crown of his head. Not deep enough to cut into the viscera, but avid enough to quell his spirit, the laceration continued to push itself into him. "Am I not yet weary enough of this wound for it to heal?" asked the man to a thing. "You are causing your wound," replied the thing. "How is this so?" asked the man. "Because you want it so much that you cannot even contain your desire for it. You have wrongly sublimated your desire for this wound into the perception of some false reality outside yourself. That world is the world of beggars for wounds and you are their king," replied the thing. "Well, that sounds a little too good to be true," replied the man. "Because all this time I thought I was the cosmos itself. Now I find out I am just a man with a wound." The thing replies: "You are and are not what you just said, are and are not a deictic lemming and immortal. YOU ARE THE COSMIC WOUND."

:::::::

Seven pounds of pain for only dollars and a few senses.

: : : : : : :

opening the speculative—
noise music on paper
the fibrousness of flesh as text
the mind-body split—
skin grafted and lupine

: : : : : : :

razing questions
locking horns
with wizards
and never
        skipping   a   beat

: : : : : : :

The end of the future of life.

: : : : : : :

Diaphanously divulge the verge of death.

: : : : : : :

Chronic sickness: the pre-implanted karmic love-touch—spinning stones and skipping lives.

: : : : : : :

That which weakens you is how strong you are.

: : : : : : :

To formulate the ineffable horror-beauty of the body through the non-language uttered vis-à-vis the mute, stiff tongue of a dead man who refuses decomposition.... through a *bog-bodied hermeticism*.

: : : : : : :

Bones are gall
stones, rolling
d
o
w
n.

: :::: : : :

The Sage of Narcissus.—A story is told by the Dead of Olde about a meeting between the sage of Narcissus, whom some thought to be a degenerate, and Narcissus' body. It is written that only Narcissus himself was present to hear the following dialogue. But oral histories have their own nuanced ways of surviving, and so the story goes....

"Listen to me. I can see people drowning in their own autoimmunity," spake the degenerate sage of Narcissus to his body.

"I see the shallow and decrepit whispers through vapors of your soul. I see the corroded muscles of your third death as they slither through the ocean waiting for birth. I saw the twelfth man behind you when he walked up to you last year, not knowing he would meet you this year. I saw you standing there before I saw you standing there, and when I told you that I knew you were there before I saw you, you gave me a look shrouded in unacknowledged fear."

His body quieted, felt itself, and then replied: "You secretly know without knowing that I am the Lord-king of all that is and is not; that I am the Plaguemaster of the heart; that I will be here before you are born and after you die your one thousand deaths. You secretly resist knowing what I truly am every time you breathe. You secretly resist knowing that I de-create your being. The floor falls, always, into your smile. You know without knowing that, beyond the sphere of the flow, there is no *No*. Cast me out! For I was forever the crooked beams in the throne of your shadow!"

: : : : : : :

The bag lady of Acheron.

: : : : : : :

And we ache.

: : : : : : :

Tristesses du corps.

: : : : : : : :

Inner Strength.—Having the courage to stay buried alive in one's own flesh in order to move *through* it.

: : : : : : : :

Without you I am W(O)RM
(Warrior (O)uroboros Repelling Matter).

: : : : : : : :

Overheard by a Warrior in the Metaphysical Foyer of Oncoming Battle.—"Scream your will into the eyes of the flesh and let no one come for you who has not known its flavors! My spirit is willing, but the flesh is weak. But I will not defile the spirit in the name of flesh. Behold all the vastness and sorrow of infinity. You will realize that this is now not your enemy, as it used to be, but in fact your closest friend!"

: : : : : : : :

The Litmus-Excoriation.

: : : : : : : :

Unthrifty.—What a waste: to waste knowing one's waste.

: : : : : : : :

Colostomies are the great ventriloquist teachers of corporeality.

Minus organs, there is no need to live in fear.

Six months in a coma will teach a person to know themselves from inside-out and Outside-in.

: : : : : : : :

The Strength of the Body.—Even strong bodies degenerate. On a spectrum of loss, healthy bodies are even more susceptible to sickness than frail ones. My body is only as useful to me as it has absolutely no use. Only when one gives up all illusions of the body's usefulness can one know the body's true uselessness, which, in effect, is its true use. This is the negative utility of the body.

: : : : : : : :

My spinal cord: the Ganges River,
exploding into the head of Shiva.

: : : : : : : :

One Must Have a Body.—For spiritual faculties to develop, one must have a body. Having a body, one simultaneously affirms and negates union with the divine, temporalizing oneness with it and casting oneself out of it and into the flesh. Without a body, one is not an historical being. But this is not to say one is *only* an historical being.

: : : : : : : :

Take No Thought of the Body.—To think of the body is to suffer. However, if, as it has been said, "thinking no-thing, will limited-self unlimit," then surely one can un-think the body—gazing at it from a clearing in the forest, from a space inside the body that is at once outside the body. Un-thinking the body curates the caress of infinity, echoing the Grand Pronouncement, "Thou are that."

: : : : : : :

The Body Has No Shape.—Against the idea of containment (of suffering, of pain), the body bursts: numinous spasms of the Outside permeate my body, revealing it as a mercurial tremor of the cosmos, a rift in the universe's coming into being. There is something distinctive about the body that attracts its own undoing, wherein cosmic magnetism and fleshy sponginess fuse into a beautiful formlessless that is the body.

: : : : : : :

The Body is in an Inverted State of Constant Bliss.—From a certain vantage, having a body causes overwhelming sadness over being an impermanent dwelling place that is not pure spirit. This is a kind of melancholy that can be broached by its own negativity, however, being a joyousness that proclaims: by having a body, I am also not this body, and by not being this body, I am also not-not this body. Thus, at the horizon of myself, I find a body in a state of bliss.

::::::::

Having a knowledge without knowing.

::::::::

It awaits us.

::::::::

Professor Hemlock returns to give his critical treatise on the Pre-Possession of the Body:

"I am pre-possessed," he begins. And the room falls silent.

"As I perceive my body, my inner gaze is already complicit within the somatico-ideological system embedded within the flesh itself: before my body ever was. But this (nervous) system is always already tied up within another autonomous system which requires my recognition to be borne into and out of; in short, I am prepossessed. That I recognize (to perceive it as "already known") the trauma signified by my body post facto does nothing to alleviate the ontological weight of the body, nor my complicity with my own nervous system. My ego's recognition of this process only serves as a mediating factor between the hidden, alternating dialectic of me and my prepossessed self. Hence, just as my body interpellated me, I—or rather, my pre-possessed self—in turn, interpellate my flesh as well (the prepossession precedes the viewing of the material body present during its own *bearing out*: the flesh itself carries the load of the world only inasmuch as I am there for it).

Let us take, for example, looking at a photograph of oneself. As I looked at a photograph of myself on the wall this morning, one taken about four years ago at a family reunion, I noticed the furtive gaze I cast at the photographer, as I tried not to "notice him." As such, my gaze was diverted there in *that moment*. But that the eyes which cast my gaze are housed within a body, the fabric, as Merleau-Ponty would say, into which the world is woven, this contingent physical body renders me producer of the world around me, in that this percept is a moment also *already known to me*. Hence, the ideology-laden semantic sign may be re-cognized, hermeneutically revalued; and yet, to some extent, I am also the producer of the materiality of the (photographed) sign onto which the "me" of the photograph has been dubbed, because it is through my senses that I can perceive the world.

My prepossessed self, however, precedes the present (photo-taking) self's being-in-the-world; it is the doppelganger forever haunting my present presence; and this doppelganger can only ever enter into an ethical encounter with its other self (me; both photo-taking-me and now-me) *after the fact*, when it has completed its future-work, establishing the entire system for me, before me. In this case prepossession precedes spontaneity, but only after it actualizes its own autonomy.

This photograph's *punctum*, to borrow a term from Roland Barthes, manifests itself for me only when I acknowledge the photograph's own Derridean, dare I say, *hauntological* repercussions not only upon my present self, but also upon the two selves functioning when the photograph was taken, the one prepossessed by the "me, myself" ideology and the other, the id(iot)logical "me"; and yet another: the spontaneous-not-yet-spontaneous self who, in that furtive glance, auto-snapped "yes" (echoing James Joyce's Molly Bloom) to that moment and thus all subsequent moments in which the photograph might be seen, called into question, or wound me."

: : : :: : ::

A Now-ledge without words.

:: : :: : ::

words cold as clay
worse than claws
harangued and the
coffin fodder

:: : : :: : :

Delinfancy.

: : :: : :: :

The world is the failed, virile cataclysm of inverted fertility.

: : :: : :: :

In the darkness of your with-holding body sits the tumor of your mindlessness.

: : : : : : : :

sharp and edges
as knives
grow inklings
and as
worst inevitable

: : : : : : : :

Novena for the veinless.

: : : : : : : :

Erupt at dusk.

: : : : : : : :

Guile and the rest of this death.

: : : : : : : :

Jejune: to be the first half of the last breath.

: : : : : : : :

Coddled to the co(a)r(s)e.

: : : : : : : :

Guttur(n)al.

: : : : : : : :

Ourobulimia.

: : : : : : : :

On Nausea.—As the great Professor Hemlock might put it, to understand the traumatic fissure one must understand its history, its production: the last way one experiences trauma will be the next way it manifests itself; it corresponds to the content and form of its own knowledge. Indeed, nausea engenders a novel, liminal, we might say, *archi-textural* design on the bio-hauntological workings of the body. Nausea points to the cave inside the body, a third space between being and non-being, but also between non-being and non-non-being, that is, a *1/3-third space* where the traumatized subject is able to connect with a human being or non-human animal according to a human-stomach reciprocity, a "gutter-nal" intuition borne out of the traumatic moment, the moment the trauma is captured in the somatic nervous system.

This reciprocity is the re-cognition of two self-consciousnesses: one) the human acknowledges that the Other acknowledges that it acknowledges it is suffering; and two) that the human acknowledges that the non-human animal acknowledges that the human acknowledges it is suffering. It is only within this intermediate 1/3-third space that the bearer of the nausea may intuit this ethic between human/Other/non-human animal. The mucosa of the bowel serves as metonymic lubricant, that which quells the vacillation between being and non-being, beginning and ending the hermeneutic mandala of gutternal empathy, reminding us that it is blood which links all animals, the *memento mori* of mammalian existence.

This blood drips at the foot of its own recognition, for not only are we reminded of the cyclical nature of mortality, but also its very structure—the mandala of empathy is symbolic of the double helix, the structure of DNA, of sentience. The double-stranded absorption in one or another's trauma comes by way of obliteration from trauma: that one cannot *feel* the other's suffering as one's own, but rather can intuit it, means that one finds rather the *obliteration of obliteration* of trauma. Here we find an unveiled self-consciousness that immanently transforms nausea into a bio-affectively transcendent category. The obliteration of trauma is not the non-existence of trauma. Rather, nausea is like the trauma of trauma. Or, rather, trauma is the nausea of nausea. Thus nausea in not the eyes of trauma, but rather it is the *eyes-in-trauma*, which synesthet(h)ically eats trauma: at its departure from the presence of trauma nausea is endowed with the non-presence of trauma, the means of its own return. The guttural g(r)aze of nausea, then, its trauma-upon-return, inhabits a place of being and non-being simultaneously, to construct an ethic that is borne out of its own passing away."

: : : : : : : :

The sum-Thing is
the knot
in your throat.

Ø

(In this moat
floats the
Divine Boat.)

PILLAR III: EXTIMACY

(Apogee Un-earthed)

: : : : : : :

Delinquent debut-taunts.

: : : : : : :

Who you are?

: : : : : : :

(N)odes to Joy.

The sonic explosions of looming privations.

: : : : : : :

Amplifying a moment of non-desire /
de-tuning non-moments of desire.

Doubling desire
as re-cognition,
if only inversely,
but forever,
and then again, and again,
into Joyousness.

: : : : : : :

X-ray Technicians.—Just when you think you're deliriously close to fooling everybody with your intelligence, usually a small child hops over to see right through you.

: : : : : : :

Vacant Vatican of the Acephalic.—To purge oneself of the papacy of the Other, from their open-handed slapping of themselves. Oneness has not hands but shoulders, and no head atop them.

: : : : : : :

The plat(t)itudinal diaphony of exorbitant levels of misunderstanding.

Misnomer standing.

: : : : : : :

Tepid telepathic trepidation.

: : : : : : :

Entropy of a Failed Telepathy.—When all one sees is other people's thoughts, one might suspect telepathy. This is a lie one tells oneself in order not to decompose. If you could actually see other people's thoughts, you would understand the misplaced univocity of the collective dereliction from the divine. "(T)here goes nothing," they secretly shout in unison.

: : : : : : :

Of course, there are other people. But there is no one here or there or even anywhere.

: : : : : : :

A Formulation for the Insistence of Recursive Self-Subversion.—One whistles their way into the others' realm, demolishing the perfection of her nothingness in order to excavate the site of the loneliness of self by saying, "Hello, here I am, remember me, the one you forgot?" In actuality, not a single one in the others' realm was the least bit errant in forgetting the singleton, for each of the others was actually the rubbish on the site itself.

: : : : : : :

Para-anamnestic awareness.

: : : : : : :

Disremember remembering the moment you could no longer remember the moment.

: : : : : : :

Against the Human/Animal Boundary.—Oliver the Chimpanzee knew several secrets as to why we perform all our melodramas. He was not taught to walk upright, but stood right up, modeling by his own behavior the gut-wrenching inevitability of a primordial love's loss. In a dream he once told me, "I loved you once, all of you, my friends. I was here for you so that you could learn from me, Humanzee the Christ Child, so that I could teach you about lost things. Just as the natives talk with wolves, I could have been your harpsichord, your synthesizer. Now my muscles have atrophied and yet another has eaten their big meal at their big table."

: : : : : : : :

peaking anamnesis/
peeking at amnesia

: : : : : : : :

Who are you? What are you becoming? (Absolutely nothing.) Don't you know you've been here before? Right there, where you sit, forever you've been there and forever you will be. Don't look in the mirror. It only shows you *glimpses* of the pitch-black mountain of non-being.

: : : : : : : :

These peaks and these valleys.

: : : : : : : :

Cosmic (n)ascent.

: : : : : : : :

A massive missive from lust to dust.

: : : : : : :

A void persists—
the recursion of your Sameness.

Nothingness,
the infinity of these blackscapes.

Disrobed by doubleness
a looking glass
neither outside nor inside.

: : : : : : :

The pangs of auto-invigor-annihilating facticity.

: : : : : : :

Besmirched in a Third Space.—Their cyber-spatial quips are mere ego trollops, scavenging for self-fostered dues. Arrest these men as scoundrels of the Other! Quips merely *delay* the libidinous hounds of desire from castrating you, pouring down w(h)ine at your intellectual crotch-parties. Alas! Your partners are lonely, sprawled out in the languished bed of your onanism.

: : : : : : :

Hedging the bet of auto-acrimonia.

: : : : : : :

Is not self-perception noetically *designed* to show how crazy you are? I doubt if tirades could ever really garner a pureness in spirit. Crazy people do not know they are crazy. But madness, madness is pure bliss!

: : : : : : :

To flail one's head into realms of dis. Headless, running about the mire as ecstatic sovereign beings, first acquiring, and then going beyond what was once lost and what is now not.

: : : : : : :

An Oxymoronic Sensibility.— Could both a friend who has never been to your town and your lifelong neighbor be behind you, scratching your back with a branch as you sit writing at the window? Of course! All is weird! In fact, you realize that the principle of sufficient reason is a magnet that attracts its own annihilation, then all things take on (and always have had) a kind of uncanny anti-gravity. Really, there is absolutely no reason to think otherwise.

: : : : : : :

Servants of sleep.

: : : : : : :

I CANNOT SLEEP IF I SLEEP WHEN I CANNOT.

: : : : : : :

None So Vile.—Dyspeptic molds grew in the corner of his consciousness, just beyond the periphery of his insight. He always knew that the maelstrom which awaited him would do so much damage that he acted as if that deep dark space did not exist. The dyspeptic molds grew and grew until one day he finally realized that not only was he so very sick that he had lied to himself, but also that, just around the corner of his self-consciousness, there were many others just like him. All identical, all so very characteristic—just little human bubbles blown from the same poisoned circular wand.

:::::::

The Traction of Inversion.—You couldn't have done what without who? Just in what way do you think anything you do has any reality whatsoever other than the reaffirmation of your own futility? Turn off, tune out, and drop into the blankness of yourself by burying your head in the ground. Stay there for no less than three years. Once three years have passed, remove the stones from around your inverted corpse. You will have become sufficiently sick of yourself to begin the True Work.

:::::::

Hear Ye, Hear Ye!.—I make a call to the Overmen of New. Come out from behind the trees that you are and walk into God. Many of the others will begin to hop on your roots to grab a free ride. Forget them. Bury them in the dust.

:::::::

The New Alchemy.—When called yellow, rip out your heart and plant it in the mire. When grown, give it to your partner and see what transpires. If they lick you up and down, you have sealed the deal. If they blacken you with ashes from your wake, you were eaten by alligators in the mire. Either way, you have de-actualized the heart to its true rubedo.

: : : : : : :

Warp-speed at the End of Days.

: : : : : : :

Moon throttling.

: : : : : : :

Sophia.—And one day, Sophia, the Queen of Stars, looked upon the congregation and said, "Today I tell you without telling you, with all I have and have not, desire and desire not, think of and think not, that we will do this until the very utter end, which, put another way, is to say that we will do this over and over again until it begins. This promise is the promise that has been handed down to me by those old ones who knew nothing at all, barring their teeth in war with time. Those antediluvian henchmen knew absolutely nothing, which is everything. They are known as the High upon High, the Dead of Olde—the Mystics of New."

: : : : : : :

Dalí on the Shore.—The great artist Salvador Dalí once famously said, "I don't need drugs. I am drugs." He is correct. Who needs drugs when we are already our own surreal ablations, these curious distortions of people lapsing within and without ourselves? If only the populace could see what cannot be seen. We would walk everywhere on water and swim in the air.

: : : : : : :

Why on earth did they flood the Akashic library? You are now beginning to understand the principle of auto-recursion within the context of madness. Madness is spiritual amazedness, the sleeplessness the saints ache to get to. Crack open a wet book and let the smeared pages dry as you read. The book will make much more sense than it did before.

:::::::

Writing my name is astro-materialized chirographical evidence that I have no name at all.

:::::::

Virility.—Thought often ejaculates itself in the hideously liminal space of writing, which is to say, writing is the bastard child of thought, the weird thing birthed from primordial ooze.

:::::::

The unrepentant doggerels
of an auto-cauterizing heart.

Sitting as the background genuflects before us,
bearing down on the beating of our being—
making us laugh.

:::::::

Butterfly reading.

: : : : : : :

Exscriptive verse hearses.

: : : : : : :

The overwhelming desire to write.... as if thought pathologically begs to transcribe itself, to *materialize* outside the ether via auto-maniculation.

: : : : : : :

Hypostatic de-creative writing.

: : : : : : :

Open up your angel wings,
and fly into the Wound.

: : : : : : :

Pre(ter)natal;
preternat(ur)al.

: : : : : : :

To enter the Wound
is to exit the womb.

: : : : : : :

Being Qua Trauma.—And there, just at the horizon, to the left of The One Who Drips with Age, and in front of He Who in His Immensity Is Larger than the Horizon, sits *The Wound*. All flows into and out of this gigantic cosmic bergschrund. It is where the Christ gnashed his teeth. And yet it is not a place at all but the pre-indictment of being—being qua trauma: this is where all life begins.

: : : : : : :

Eternal, eternatal;
Eat-urn-All;
Et(ur/n)atal.

: : : : : : :

The rift in between being born undead and the funeral of consciousness.

:::::::

Murmur of the Amplifier.— The riff/rift in your head is deeper than the gash that severed it from your neck. The gigantic crevasse of *The Wound* does not encompass a distance between two points, but rather amplifies the mouthed murmurings of absolute bewilderment: the riff/rift is the smile on the face of your sweet, cephalophoric melon.

:::::::

An Important Distinction.—Why put so much emphasis on relegating suffering to a particular temporality? This seems to be a sin. Should it not be just as easy to displace that suffering onto eternity? Why be held down?—it is a strange thing that eternity does not become the immense repository of despair rather than temporality.

:::::::

Towards an Absolute Suffering.—Your "sickness unto death," as Kierkegaard would put it, is that you relegate your suffering to a here and now, while the anagogic truth of the matter is that the here and now is actually eternity (one not limited by your shroud of false keeping). Consciousness of suffering must be transmuted into a non-knowledge of suffering. In other words, one should not/cannot reduce suffering to a form of knowledge. Rather, it must be released into to its own entirely excessive freedom. We must let suffering free, to enact its Holy Rites, to be itself, sovereign, to reign. We must always implore—cultivate, tend to, be on the side of—an *absolute* suffering.

: : : : : : : :

Melting Away.—To suffer freely in a way that does not constitute more endless suffering, but to accept suffering as immanent self-melting.

: : : : : : : :

Infinitely Domesticated.—Kaleidoscopic, wrought in flesh, we are kept as the ether's pets.

: : : : : : : :

Magmus of Indigo Addressing the Predisposse.—You are the Formica to my Redwood. Mice burrow into your pulp-pits of self, while the Owl of Minerva takes up its home upon my three-thousandth branch. I am the throne of fossilized wood and the saw which cut it. Impenetrable, strong, deader than the density of dark matter— *consciously* moving in between existence and non-existence at will is the absolute paradigm of self-lessness.

:::::::

the cold intensity of warmth
the warmth of cold intensity

:::::::

The lightness of a bearable non-being.

:::::::

Never bemoan the transgression zone.

:::::::

A weird materiality preceding your existence by several thousand aeons and is thus Now.

: : : : : : : :

Eyes without a Face.—There was a certain group of people (a microcosm of the lot of people, actually), who, when looked at, revealed not their faces but only the veneer of vacated tufts of goo. The world became slime in their presence. Their eyes, puncture wounds, burrowed holes into the soulless vacuums of themselves. Seven billion walking wounded.... straddling deliverance and birth rites.

: : : : : : : :

Fresh Air.—Caustic, ironic, mellifluous and disingenuous, they arose from their adult cradles. If only they knew how a morning walk could correct their slipped discs!

: : : : : : : :

On the Defensive.—To narrate one's life within a teleological bubble of self-aggrandizement is merely the defense mechanism of a persona devoid of the sacred, of one who is forgotten of Void.

: : : : : : : :

Oracular, the skies—
heavens and hells
weep for your return
to Paradise.

: : : : : : : :

Behind consciousness.

: : : : : : : :

Aloof,
but not stale.

: : : : : : : :

Enough Already.—Give it up! How are you supposed to move on when you sit aloof, stale, unconsciously gazing at (without dissecting) the very entrails that told you of your formidable existence?

: : : : : : :

On the Operating Table.—I opened up my ribs for the return of the universe within. Extracted is my heart, all for the presence, through absence, of a new life-without-flesh in flesh. I am the hearing of the wind, a preternatural whisper fornicating with ear drums, a sly mercurial touch across your skin.

: : : : : : :

Outdoorsmen.—A solitary, rather than an attitudinal, encampment helps to keep the bogeyman at bay. Set fire to self, fanning flames of bliss into your maddened sail. Recesses once harbored and unknown even to your journey's daemon will open into infinity. Remember: bogeymen are wolves in human clothing, imposing attitudinally their weight as an anchor on your individuation. But no amount of attitude will advance upon the encampment of a pure solitude.

: : : : : : : :

Genuine is the grove worm.

: : : : : : : :

Those of Olde have listened closely, evoking black plasma to wash themselves, and joining, through spiritual cleansings, with the eternal.

: : : : : : : :

Drawn and Quartered.—Life draws me out from the extremities of itself. I genuflect, letting myself be decapitated by its very vicissitudes, by the origin of the extreme.

: : : : : : : :

Hyperbawlick.

: : : : : : : :

Awaken from Slumber.—I walk along pale shores of melancholia, awaiting splendors of darkness, zeal in disproportion, and quietude during irreverent mornings.

: : : : : : :

Thrice Born.—Carry the suffering, offer it to the toads of the mire, give them the drugs of false hope, and be gone. As you walk away, be sure to caress the onyx foot of the bog body. You were buried twice. The third time will be the finality, the beginning of reversing the advanced lethargy of infinity.

: : : : : : :

Abandon All Life.—Done with pretense, abandoned of life, I floated like a buoy out of the aeon's mist.

: : : : : : :

Nameless Cities.—Wyrd: your Nemo is resurrected and unable to speak… the fate of lions entrenched in your cities.

: : : : : : :

the negative utility of regimen /
the utility of unregimented negativity

The infinite obliteration of temporality via the spontaneous and ecstatic reversal of once-Sisyphean labors.

:::::::

Goosebumps.—Did you hear that howling wolf? Did he wake you? Let him spoil you with the gift of self-contemplation. For when the moon goes down you will have already forgotten what you suddenly realized. *You must not go back to sleep.*

:::::::

The presence of the pretense of the fear of your elderly self's own grimace towards you.

The inexorable quiddity of negativity.

:::::::

Glitched to the nines.

: : : : : : :

Looking in the other room to see a stranger bending over and not knowing how they got there or who they were. Realizing it is you; it is you looking at yourself in the other room.

: : : : : : :

A laughter laughing.

: : : : : : :

Furtive Smiles.—Idiosyncrasies, quirks, making jokes in the mornings—when laughter simultaneously erupts due to two dissimilar senses of humor who realize, in that hybrid moment, that amusement often proceeds from existential despair, and that existential despair is not all that bad because it implies that nothing is really any more important than anything else. That is a kind of laughter: the amusement at knowing that you are insufferably alive and that being alive can be deadly beautiful.

: : : : : : :

Juggler of Flowing Rivers.— I once walked past a man who was running on a trail while juggling three balls. We briefly looked at one another. He didn't see me; *he saw himself looking at me*. This is the type of detached awareness for which one ought to strive.

: : : : : : :

On Those Who Eat in Their Car.—There is an abounding and overemphasized false sense of community in human society. To have known more people who eat take-out in their cars than those like the businessman who just walked into a 3 Star restaurant; and for one to have no less compassion for the businessman than for the one eating in their car. At the very least, the those eating in the car direct their will into a *zone of comfortability*—of an easing to their pain—whereas this particular businessman hardly knows he is in it! Ignorance is blasé. Yet his suit is as taut as the ascetic's garter belt of wiry mesh. Self-doubt and suffering are at both ends of their spectrum, and the world is the pendulum of this spectrum.

: : : : : : :

Explosi(e)ve.—To explode self-perception and drain into magnanimity of Self-realization.

:::::::

To be free of them is to free them.

:::::::

Let Them Do What They Want.—To stand only with those who can stand with themselves is to lay with those who are always already laid down.

:::::::

Flip the House of Being (Verödung's Lament).—Let the tears slowly glide out of your well-worn eyes. Those are the eyes of true beauty: those pitch-black realms that house the purest nothingness. The world feeds them with all that is and is not world, just as the multiverse carves out a small place for you to attest to its unfathomability. Enter into the multiplicity of yourself and pull the innards out of your mouth. Stay put and let loose. The inverse is the folded reality of Reality.

:::::::

Hill Worm.—Purpurescent and purple, seeing from atop my hill-body, [purp-oselessly] spellbound by the inchoate complicities of every-One's hidden whispers to and with[out] the Outside, I hear/here the hulk-end nature of your sulking, underground slithering. Feed us, unto you, sweet grove worm. You are the nightmare-spawn of death's chthonic head—the germination of glowing wheatgrass stifling a curmudgeon's forest-throat.

: : : : : : :

Spectropoeitic flâneury.

: : : : : : :

Bubbled and thriving, unwinding from the Cosmic Wound, walks the silent ghostshifter of being's utter(ed) end. Tremorizing in terror, in terra firma waves of potshots from grassy knolls, punctured by bullets' flesh and search-seizing via the mind's dual heart-hearth. Bays of pig's breath and incandescent dew dreamers ejaculate milk-end droplets, letting some pass but not letting them Goethe their own way. Seasoned and pickling, the sun's rays as watchful odes to the prickling, loving tenderness of the Moon's thoughtful touch.

:::::::

(Courageous—

but

for what?)

Pillar IV: Flagrancy

(Teratogenesis
of the
Stood-Still Hierophant)

: : : : : : :

The electromagnetic speculum.

: : : : : : :

The Orifice of Consciousness in the Spreading of the Bicameral Mind's Eye.

: : : : : : :

Igne natura renovatur integra.—Allow yourself to be fully engulfed in the fire of the death of your own falsity. The fire through which you die is the flame by which you will eternally live.

: : : : : : :

Gerrymeandering.

: : : : : : :

Two sylphs divulge in the woods.

I took the path-less travel dawn.

:::::::

Echocardiogrammar.

:::::::

SpaceHeart.—It is from the Space of the Heart that I stand. Uncannily, the divine vapors exude from the flesh, much like the gentle droplets of milk flow from the teats of a feral cat feeding her newborn litter. This is the litter of outcasts, the litter of the undomesticated, wherein it is not the unruly temptations of modernity that blink the eyes, but rather the shrill and erotic screams of pure, vacuous fucking. A hunger persists in these woods. And only seven of the twelve will eat tomorrow. But it is still from the space of the Heart that I stand.

:::::::

breadcrumbing backwardly
losing the non-way home

not moving by not not moving
to meander, always, as such

: : : : : : :

being unbound

unbeing bound
(by desire)

bound unbeing
(in the mire)

unbound being

: : : : : : :

Verminculcators.

: : : : : : :

Wormed.—A tragedian at heart, and caustic and ironic, the worm fatefully cut itself in half due to its fear of the plow. The worm then looked up and saw that on one side of the sky was darkness and the moon, and on the other side of the sky was the sun and light. The worm cried out, "You offending criminals. Have I not delivered myself to you each day of my life, digging wormholes into your cosmos?" The moon held the sun's hand and told him thus: "You are the worm of a mighty crevice, the crevice of our hive mind. Do not fear, young one. You will grow back together, backwardly." This was the truth. The worm grew back together backwardly, with both parts of his stomach facing outward and his eyes in his ass. Yet he was never happier, never so keen in spirit and mind. For in a disjointed body, all is compelled into inversion. The worm had found serenity in the amputated and inverted Ouroboros of itself.

: : : : : : :

Improvisation-All.

: : : : : : :

Intuition.—To meet a Grecian Thing called daimon. Sitting upon the shoulder of Socrates, it whispers to those of Olde how to access the sprawling juxtapositions of non-desire.

: : : : : : :

Oh Darkness, This Darkness.—I sat among the trees

contemplating my life. Saturn walked by, as if not realizing that I was sitting there. I then remembered that we had moved on from each other; that he had taught me all he could. When I entered Neptune, Saturn wept a tear. Saturn is always crying tears of individuation. Saturn is my friend of friends. He misses me. Now if only Pluto would let me enter, I would introduce him to Saturn. But Saturn would still not understand. Saturn cannot come with me, and he is sad.

:::::::

Harpooned.—Do not fear the raven's head. The fluttering of its wings: a harp evoking the sounds of your illusion's distillation.

:::::::

Fruit of the Wound.

:::::::

Be Leary of Them.—Tenacity holds a role in the strength of your grip, entrusting a void between the rock and the hard place. Even their candy will become sour in your presence; even the trees will lose their leaves. I say this not to scare you, but to warn you of the others who will not respect the fidelity you have to your fearlessness—to the utter, naked, cosmic event that is you.

:::::::

A Salutation Concerning Mourning.— Spawned from the visit of an acosmic twirl in the brain, a Voice whispers "Valhalla, Valhalla, Valhalla..." When I returned, I said to myself, "What do you think *this* is? Life?!"

:::::::

Ungripped,
let go of,
and hurled

over the edge
of worldliness.

:::::::

Revelry.—An extravaganza! In complete celebration of baseness, to rummage through the sale of self-longing, to create a new being, a human who exists without world, who upholds the utmost transgressions of the self. The Buddha will smile in amazement that we have ended the hallucination of ourselves.

:::::::

Puerile Rain Fell.—Person A: "Gibberish is only as useless as it is desensitizing." Person B: "Contempt is only as immoral as it is untruthful." Those are apt if one grants them the accord of cliché en masse. But, as it were, what is puerile about those statements is not their semantics, but rather the *vehicle of their ideation*. Person A has made the dangerous error of attributing utility an affective quality. Person B upholds herself as a purveyor of the law. But wouldn't it be so much more apt if these ethical pupils' first thoughts were ontologically about their minds. I doubt they would ever speak another word in sheer fear of susceptibility to the insatiable non-Euclidean candor of the Outside.

: : : : : : :

hologrammer
hollow grammar
halo programmer

: : : : : : :

The ontology of the inside of a saint's cocoon: the dawning of a halo, or the phenomenology of a halo-as-it-dawns.

: : : : : : :

When we consent to the taking place of language we consent to negation's abysmal dwelling place, disclosing the possibility of an affirmative "yes."

: : : : : : :

unpurposed proportions
proprio(per)ception
inversely proportional

: : : : : : : :

The gravi(nvi)tation of the non-center.

: : : : : : : :

Becoming Varmit.—We have heard the rumors. An elephant of laziness rests in your general vicinity. Jolt it! Become the mouse of eternity. Time is not a space. Your head is not a receptacle but a disseminator. Dog will hunt. Mouse will wander.

: : : : : : : :

A Distinction.—"Living a good life": what one thinks they are doing. "Walking on one's hands backwards on a collapsed stage in which mute actors clownishly mime their own births": what one is actually doing.

: : : : : : : :

(Psst… those clothes are wearing people.)

:::::::

Legless, Treading Water.—There are no feet attached to the lugubrious legs of the Wanderer. Under liturgical duress, the Soul weeps waters of aeons. Unable to tread, he will sink to the earthen core. That is, unless the Soul sheds enough tears to float him to the top of the mountain.

:::::::

Shrunken Heads.—Spot him. Corner him. Adumbrate the wounds through the blackened puttering of his mind. Then detach yourself from the Dwarf of Thought—he has been trapped in the auto-corrugating chasm of dysmorphia, diminishing the size of everything. You must annunciate your arising.

On the Loose.—Once the Dwarf of Thought has been let loose, he will speak these words: "Alas! I have come from beyond to show you that you are nothing. Never were, never will be, anything. And now you will weep at the absolute freedom of it all. You are nowhere. Forget it." Without you, the dwarf is a giant.

:::::::

Identity hedonist.

:::::::

Living to Eat.—Three men sat among one another, talking, over lunch. A beautiful old woman who had obtained the fountain of youth entered, but they did not take notice. Sitting at the table next to them, she overheard their laughter. It was the curious and mitigated laughter of the failure of death. For, death itself could not reap from these men their image of a life. (Life hath no passivity like a contagious ignorance of oneself.) Inconsolable, they fill up the empty hallways of infinity with their own clownish projection-manifestations.

:::::::

Burning and at stake.

Forgive me of myself.

:::::::

Bleak: the absent caress of a feeling.

Hot: the tingling skin of matter.

Derided: the withering latching onto history via the fogged lens of an identity.

:::::::

Butcher's Best Advice.—A young woman once kissed a retired lawman on the cheek after he told her something remarkable. "Throughout the history of human civilization, there were only ever three good men: Christ, Buddha, and the neighborhood butcher." She replied, "You are clever, but you do not make any sense." Then she asked him, "Tell me, why was the butcher such a good man? Did he not see how horrible the world has become?" The lawman replied, "Butchers work magic with the dead. Butchers tell no lies."

:::::::

A Coup for Thriving Hearts.—Tidying up the undying

layer of mud between spoken sentences is about as filthy a task as paper towels absorbing formaldehyde from a leaking corpse. But that's not to say people don't intend to mean what they say. In fact, perhaps spoken words are the verbal embodiment of a pure nihilism, of a meaninglessness that persists at the behest of a long-lost earnestness.

: : : : : : :

All-seeing.—The thread of my inexistence winds down, down, into the black hole of your perfectly cataracted eyes.

: : : : : : :

A Misunderstanding.—So many times I wandered up to the windowsill of your ardor, only to be shown by the animals that you did not dwell in that house.

: : : : : : :

Loveless.—I once called forth love from a mythic fountain of blankness. But you were still so unaware and lofty and full of gall.

: : : : : : :

Atoned.—You gave me away to the lemmings. And after I vanquished them, after I had escaped, I came back to dispel your wily oath to Maya.

: : : : : : :

The Sickness unto "Life".—I saw three of them sitting there, their backs against the grains of pine, attempting to walk out of their coffins, but unable—because of their verisimilitude to inexistence—to move even an inch. Just then, as the sounds of the gnashing wood goat reached a fever pitch, a worm crawled out of the second coffin and whispered thus: You are the One, crawl out of yourself, you nameless goat of nine. I replied: What are you? How is it that you are able to speak? The worm replied thus: I am of the Olden Throne. We speak in whispers to the stones and the flowers, but only in dire times do I speak out loud. I am here to raise you out of yourself so that you may truly live. I replied: I do not understand you, but you say things that are so strange that they pique my interest. How is it that I may live? The worm replied thus: You must become completely sick, even sicker than you presently are, and vomit yourself up to the complete freedom of oblivion.

:::::::

Below
the
bottom.

:::::::

A Worm of One's Own.—Carelessly, a man sat on a stoop in the corridor of his own misgivings. There was no shelter there, and it was an ignominious stain on his "hierarchy of needs." For what seemed like aeons, a worm painstakingly crawled its way up to the stoop. It said to the man: "You need to reverse this thing you call yourself." The man cringed and wriggled. After nine minutes, he sat up and proceeded to walk out into the desert of thought. After seven years, the man came back. He glowingly hovered above the stoop in the corridor. The worm returned, staring in amazement. The man thanked the worm for its teachings. Then, he reached into his belly button and pulled out the universe. Twenty-one galaxies, the Baoding balls of his existence, floated in his hands. He said to the worm: "I once sat on this stoop as a derelict of the divine. You, worm, are a saint." He then put both hands into his belly button, pulling his flesh wide away from the cosmic opening of himself to reveal his sacrum to the worm. The worm entered this sacral dimensional space, an immense pyramid wherein inside the world is and outside houses the tomb of the man's former life. The point of the pyramid points inwards and sits on the point of itself, sucking itself out of itself like the look of the sound of an octahedral bee buzzing about its own hivemind. "What was once an ignominious stain on his hierarchy of needs is now a sacral pathway into pyramidic self-evisceration," thought the worm. At the top of this triangular apex of the inner world sits failure; this is the accord of all who have been born into the world. It will remain. And at the bottom of this apex is self-actualization. It is reserved for those who have walked out of the into, and into the out of, that is, have reversed failure vis-à-vis being absolutely squeezed by it. Diamonded, failure's reversal is actualized by pulling itself through itself. The worm sat, awe-struck, as stars twinkled. "You can stay if you want," said the man to the worm. The worm acquiesced, and the man closed back up his body. He walks among us, worm inside, as a living token of the Eternal.

: : : : : : : :

Agony—

existential
anagogy

this thrownness
into and
from atop

the
Geworfenhei(gh)t

: : : : : : : :

A Room of Undoing.—The elders in the community often spoke of an old dreadlocked sage who was brought into prison. He never said a word to anyone. But one night, as the sage slept deeply in his room, a guard heard these words being whispered from the sage's unmoving mouth:

"I know a room, a room *you* cannot enter. I know this room from the inside-out. It took me a long time to find my way into it, and now that I'm there, I wish not to leave. It is so cozy; at once intimate, comfortable, and yet large enough to fill a universe. But just as you see this room from the outside-in, not yet able to walk in, I have a restraint as well. I cannot open the door to the outside. That door must be opened by one who has found the key. Until then, I will keep the windows clean, so that an onlooker's gaze can view the inside of this beautiful room. At this time of year, the windows will surely be dirtied by sandstorms. But they must. What else can a window be other than itself, an eternal passageway that, like Janus, looks inward and outward at the same time, beckoning the senses to become what they were meant to be, instruments of divinity."

The guard continued his service until one day, long after the old sage had died, he earned his retirement papers. The people in his community were surprised when he opened a small shop fixing windows. It is said that he charged no one for his services.

:::::::

Somatic memory casting call.

::::::::

The gravity of "the end of history" as a meontological category.

::::::::

The metaphysical identification with misidentifying the excessive scent of an old woman's synthetic perfume.

::::::::

Hammered Dulcimer.—There was a man who usually sat on the steps of a nearby mosque. Each day at noon the neighborhood children would hurry over to watch him, for it was said that he entered ecstatic trances, pithily tapping his feet against the ground in tsunamis of sonic finesse. "He's the reincarnation of Fred Astaire!" said one child. "It's pure magic," said a mother as her daughter eagerly tugged her down the street. There was a whimsical nature to the man's so-called tap dances, a spontaneity of love and light. And yet there was also a harsh decanted pitch, a self-knowingly grave redundancy—the recurring diurnal racket of thin steel trouncing concrete. This second racket mutely hammered its way into the onlookers' third eyes like an immense invisible hummingbird bustling about a thousand microphones. For, underneath the ground upon which the sage dazzled the crowd, and of which they could not see, was the crypt of his former life—a dark den of misguided logic, the unkempt bed of a clown whose pierced neck tells the stories of an unmitigated circus of social vampirism. He hammered the ground, sweating, tap, tap, tapping away in delirious fits of preternatural ecstasy. In and out and out and in.... oh, the circular vortexes, figure eights of abyssal lucidity. He had to wake himself up. One day, which is to say, right Now, he would unhinge that old heirloom chandelier upon his unaware self's inter-dimensional head.

:::::::

Mouth of Disgust.—That man yaps vapidly and in excess.... a Pac-Man with limbs, he inhales the perpetual reanimation of himself in order not to die, snorting cocaine through the deviated septum of failed masculinity.

:::::::

The vitriol of a glowworm needn't be regulated. Nor should it be relegated.

: : : : : : : :

Manich(ald)ean Gnosti(s)c(h)ism.

: : : : : : : :

Mythomaniacal, one sees not All, but all of Maya.

: : : : : : : :

A Silhouette.—The weeping singularity of a stood-still identity.

: : : : : : : :

Blurring the Gap.— Drowned out, like an ant's ear drums (having not yet "ears to hear" in order to "listen and understand"), as it sits, uncertainly, on a twig placed atop the crevice between a washing machine and a dryer, is our consciousness of Consciousness. The twig is also a razor's edge, on which the ant balances itself, and in which lurks the seed of the failure of gravity. On one side of the razor's edge the ant enacts faith upon its future, knowing in full measure that it will not fall if it maintains (via will) the clarity of balance.

On the other side of this razor's edge, however, sits the unknown permeability of caprice, the strange undoing of the twig by the unevent of the opposite of sound, a gone-poof where the ant's lack of ear drums has nothing at all to do with anything.

This caprice lets loose the will's nonsensical parody of itself and asks skeptical questions of it pertaining to hidden biological functions, hereditariness, what happens inside a vessel of blood, etc. This nothing at all to do with anything is actually a something, but a sum-Thing that does not require one's active thinking of it to be anything. Is this something then a nothing? And could it not also be said to be the wyrd relationship an individual might, quite unsuspectingly, that is, ignorantly, have *with oneself*, as one peers into the tilted mirror of being to see something so bewildering that the experience of this being-fuddled becomes a comico-frightening endeavor, one which promises nullity but secretly vows erasure?

Ultimately, one must balance oneself on this twig, but in such a way as to simultaneously remove the twig's being-as-precept, to exhort the blurring of the gap between oneself and the world and of the crevice's acosmic blurring of world and world. Blurring the gap dispels the incisive derision of identity, of the plugging up of the ineffable, of the fear of falling. Make not love with the succubus that indicts and invites the mirror of being's reflection, but rather with the one that calls it into question.

If one would only realize that one is always already the deaf ant…. that our ear drums resign us to a certain mode of consciousness in which fear itself is the ultimate, illusive sound….

: : : : : : :

(Synesthesia Obscura) ((Epistolic Svanati))

(((Aura(l) Intonata)))

: : : : : : :

Bloodhound moaners,
gleaning-loafing on the razor's edge;
stage diving into sandstorms;
stalking prey like a
fin de siècle grizzly.

: : : : : : :

Glanced.—The lightning quick tiger-pinch of a Kung-Fu master in the thralls of ego death.

: : : : : : :

Uncanny resemb(a)lance.

: : : : : : :

Holding out for no one.

: : : : : : :

Today is a good day to die before you die!

: : : : : : :

And you cannot find your face.

Interlud(Ic): Opus Gregorius

(Public Oration at 45 Feet)

"I wonder what he's thinking about?" asked a young woman in the small crowd standing around the pillar.

: : : : : : :

He overheard her, and he said.. did you know my name? back then I had a name.. back then.. over there: (*Pointing*) over there.. right there, pointing.. right there, *pointing*—I—had a name.. over there.. back there/ back then.. right *there*.. Riiiiight *there*.. almost.. right THERE.. yes—in front of us.. right there—in the front of behind me.. back there.. NO [[here]].. here—right NOW.. yes, sure.. pssst—I.. *Sure*.. no—I.. *I* had a name, no?

Remember? Yes/no/?

My town called me Gregory and all was well with everything, except that nothing ever was anything other than what I always thought it was, and, so tell me, how could that have ever been?! Ha!! And so I watched. I just watched.

I watch. Nothing other than utter non-identification with what is watched. Is watchful. Watching nothing other than neither nothing ever was, and—Oh, the joy!—Oh, such joys here are there. Such joys—are. The joy. Is everywhere, is neither nothing than not ever. Joy! Aha! Ha! Aha! Joy—

so this right here.. then : : : : : : : right there, (*almost*) : : : : : : : is, must be, is not, really ought never to be.. but is.. is nothing other than the utter undeath of the opposite of absolute total strife.. the birthing.. of joy, the birth only ever.. of joy.. the piecing together of those—"the these"—(and with[out of] the purest ease).. reversed preternatural un-moments of dis-ease.. here "I" is not.. not here or there or anywhere, but Everywhere—always never, or before.. and not.. or ever.. ever always is—only never..

this ethereal pit of nothing: : : :
: : :/
ever: : :
: : : :
everything ever/

I see you. Who, "me"?

I see me standing over
there, right
before I never saw you.
And it is there that is
never. And it is there that
everything happens not.
Not ever. And always
ever. Forever. Always and
ever, for not anything.
Is nothing. Right right
before it all starts, nil,
and right right, nil, after
it, nil, nil, never even ever
never began—

and when it is.. and is not.. is not and is not not ever.. everything will always already be.. just as it never was before.. just as it never was.. before you thought of it.. and un-think it.. as we speak.. have spoken.. and are speaking.. of.. it..

NOW? Yes/no/?

So I met it there. This
thing is me,
and I must beware... to
call it home... or call
it something other than
home—

never always is.. not.. not is not ever never Now.. is not not Now never even? hardly.. all is spinning there.. but it's not here.. nor neither there.. that this kiss of love shows Love to me.. for *I* am not this thing "I see".. and when Love comes.. it comes from Thee.. this thing that is.. but is not me—complete..

Androgyny,

Androgyne of all Splendor
Of all Splendors
All splendors
ALL splendors,
Here I am. Come and take me.

and the Godhead.. is (t)here.. and definitely.. not there.. and not not there.. either.. waiting/never waiting.. in an

Instant.. that never.. was anything.. other than something.. other than it all-ways already was.. not.. and is.. and cannot be anything other.. than that which.. is never.. never not.. and not to begin with.. not even ever..

And so it
begins,
and so
here
is end.
This
Love is
every-
thing
and
nothing,
which
ends,
before,
before
after
it all
starts,
and nev-
er was,

ever, nor
ever was
never,
nor even
was
before—

a l l splen dor s.. and at that point.. the point pointing at its difference.. when I caught myself : : : : : :there: : : : : : : falling.. pineally.. through the air.. the air which has no gravity.. no pit, nor life, nor non-life neither.. that is where the non-there calls.. and that is where All never not falls.. for in the idleness of sleep.. something loving somewhere.. nowhere nothing that loves.. but loves still.. is ever-loving.. is not.. is only ever nothing.. nothing other than.. Love..

And it whispers:

And Maya I will
not obey.
Maya, I will
not obey. Not in
sleep, nor wake,
nor death. Not in
life, nor dream,
nor breath. Not

in not and not in
other, and naught
ever nothing is
ever-so-neither—

And the wisps heard: *This is All and All is All.*
And All is all
that All can be,
neither nothing
and everything
is, not, and All
is not this thing
I am, and is not
anything other
than. All is all
and All is All…
not. And All is
nothing other
than neither, and
neither is noth-
ing other than all
and everything.
All is All and All
is All, not. All is
All. All is. Not.

All. All is All.
ALL

..they used to call me Gregory..
..somatic memory
.recalled.
released..

..gregarious Gregorius..
—Remember?

Joy—
is y/ours
joyous
—Jo/y/ou(r)s

Part Two: Stylinau(Gh)T

(Mission Specialist
Pseudo-Isambardo
Of Toporas)

Pillar V: Keeper

(Spiritual Tunnels)

:::::::

"I now dub thee Mission Specialist Pseudo-Isambardo of Toporas."

:::::::

I have had other names before Now,
but I cannot recall any of them.

:::::::

Born into a last name deictic, which points at my-Self as the hinge of this diptych.

:::::::

Incumbent fumbling.

:::::::

Alchemical exhortations.

:::::::

Planetary tinctures.

:::::::

Orbital exhaltations.

:::::::

Sighs of re-animators.

:::::::

Relief scapulae.

:::::::

Roux of Souls.—I remember, long before my birth, I sat, unwashed, in a pool of souls—each one of us perfect, unadulterated, made of pure light. When I was born my own thrownness into being performed autotelic deeds unto the flesh. I had a voice—could speak my name. I must now ask of myself, "Why? Why did you cast yourself out? Why such masochism?" When once was not and not was whence, from this point I must deliver, through the dim caskets of time, my own life unto Thee. Take me back to the place of light, to see the liver in my body, to feel the lightness of your Oneness in the roux of souls. From that place I will be unborn, and the others, sitting, naked, in the pools of Lethe, will come with Thee to speak thy Name.

:::::::

grasping for one's head—
gasping at the realization

when the kundalini pops…

Begotten of a sudden,
sphere-like and enamored of.

Fond indifference—
a loving detachment.

:::::::

Forever and a lot.
        Fazed and diffused.
                Spontaneous undulating glowing.

: : : : : : :

Flabbergast(h)ing.— As a young man, the old dreadlocked sage once came across an unsightly Thing in the woods. The Thing whispered to him:

“Have you ever known that all of your words are completely useless if you cannot attribute to them the non-experience of a divinity so vast that its own incommunicability becomes its manner of suspension (of dis-belief), where the love of its lostness and the lostness of its love combine to form one ubiquitous, auto-flagellating Word, *the* Word, the One to which your lofty unborn gaze draws itself. This cataclysm of utility marks your dereliction from the divine, that ontological slaughterhouse in which you place your trust, confining you to the horizon where cosmic thought is banished by your own reptilian nature.

Think about this, and then swiftly forget it: non-thinking is the only way out of this reprehensible hologram of yourself. The world is purely world until it becomes other than itself, just as you are merely you until you are other than yourself, which is to say, not you and not-not you, but rather what is you when the is *is not*.

You are dwarfed by your own incomprehensibility. Step outside, which is really inside, and then reverse the outside to be inside and the inside to be outside. This Outside-Inside is the negativity of the All, and once you reverse the reversal you may be granted entrance into the eternal darkness that is your shimmering light."

The old man never told the Thing that he was in fact deaf, and just nodded. Though one day, many years later, after many trials and tribulations, he watched himself (as if from atop a hill) pass his younger self on the street. The man stared, bewildered. His younger self winked, mutely mouthed hello to him, and walked off into the sun-lit city. At that moment, the old man heard and understood exactly what the Thing had told him.

:::::::

The auto-futural immanence of a wink.

:::::::

...moving behindness.

pointedly forward...

:::::::

trapped inside a cube/
being crucified by Being

:::::::

Crucifixionarium.—At the brink of an inkling, the slaughter of a rejected moment, I failed to grasp the *that I am*. Bring me to You—through the sedentary fixation of duration cast as shadow, the rust of a nine inch nail. Crucifixionarium, (non)viewing place of the weird materiality, thy innards of old inhabit Thee.

:::::::

Cannot not not know
not not knowing,
at least.

:::::::

a hint of new life,
bridging over
the toxic sludge moat

Castling.

A spark!
Ancient and unfamiliar,
elevating soul—
a fond uncanniness.

:::::::

Resurrection Day.—I cannot say I have felt this sort of energy before: at once defamiliarizing and strong, I feel awakened to some weird level of cryptic consciousness, a place that I should not be and, yet, feel welcome. There are others here—but few. There is a shade of white behind the façade, a glowing and prismatic softness that's energy is piercing. I cannot claim to contain the creative impulse found at the foot of the unknown wash that survives behind me (that is, beyond the limits of the front of me). I am not 'I' here, but rather the distended reversal of a catatonic thought, the 'who I thought I was'. The Voice of an unknown flesh beyond flesh penetrates my body, raising it (that is, sinking it) further outwards, to worship the exuberance of this white energy. I am an unknown to me; Tat Tvam Asi. My God (is) I AM. Everything, in all its unfamiliarity, has brought me to the most condensed form of energy regarded thus far.

: : : : : : :

Noise—

the occult scion
that curates the scission
between self and world

guarding the penultimate location
where wyrd becomes itself,
long before the world becomes world

: : : : : : :

The anxious la-mentality of limin(im)ality. The gut-wrenching laxative of thought as it unwinds the mind's own correlates. This anxiety: reason's abortion; the liminality, an exhortation.

: : : : : : :

Between the brinks
        and the inkling.

: : : : : : :

The soul as auto-interdimensional-ocutor.

: : : : : : :

enter the tunnel
(just for a moment)

: : : : : : :

Green is a rose.

: : : : : : :

The thoracic spark of the plentitude of the Heart.

: : : : : : :

Shown in green hue
and through the heart chakra
a four-leaf clover
which sits before me.

: : : : : : :

Alive in the Bardo.—In this moment of deepening, skin is raised, sucking into myself the world-in-itself. I speak of this as lived experience, one characterized by the union of this etheric clover with my consciousness. But I must also say that I think I am seeing all this backwards. I do not think that I sucked the world-in-itself into my being. Rather, it seems, in the negativity of cosmic revelation, I saw what-is-there-but-is-not-there-*for-me*: the merging of the hauntological with the *for-itself*; the realization of the "when you get there, there is no *there* there," conjoined with the *that I am*.

: : : : : : :

Have you ever spoken a word that was not yours? Have you in fear caressed the unspeakable horror of divinity?

: : : : : : :

A paddy wagon of pewter urns.

: : : : : : :

Oblivionized.—Beyond the oblivion of my grey wake, I rest inside a nested egg. An egg so soft, an egg so kind, now sits crushed as Humpty's spine. If he'd have known, he would not rise. He has not been shown; he is not yet wise. Beyond the excrement, there is nothing foul. Beyond oblivion is nothing now. Come with me and we will see that nothingness is the gift of three: Father of the phantom elf, he is gifted with the love of Hell. Son of the Holy Three, send Him home, he's not ready. Holy Ghost of Arche-Fossil, give them the cover of Lord Colossal. Elohim of the beyond, show me that I can't respond. Never gracing the polymorphic phantom-whore called Life, I call into the abysmal crevice of my mind. It calls back: "You were not even here yet."

:::::::

the voidic thrust
of my heart
seeing itself as world

thinning and
immanent

: : : : : : :

What might the juncture say about the plane?

: : : : : : :

Passaging.—In a tunnel, sloshed and thick, the passage between 'what was once' and 'what is not' holds being at bay—becoming is bitter now, hollow. Rather, the passage is hollow, existence staggers through the passage. (cosmos → body ← passage). The passage (on the horizontal plane) simultaneously exists (vertically) *above* materiality and *below* the limits of temporal context, and *below* materiality and *above* the limits of temporal context. It's not within and it's not without, and it's not-not within and it's not-not without. It is cosmic contingency. Through the black hole is the white hole is ass-hole of the temporal. Passage is sphincter, wormhole of the future. Unclenched, I am reminded: You are not alone; you are not not alone. Staggering, I yield: "Hello."

: : : : : : :

The earth is a queer round wand,
nothing but a gleaming non-comprehensiveness.

: : : : : : :

become
the
OeCtEhAeNr

: : : : : : :

Cannot see straightness,
convolutedly unwavering.

: : : : : : :

Vision.—A positive perception folds into spacetime, unfolding an autonomous negative perception and dropping it down a funnel. Shifting this perception from the forefront to the background, this relationship announces its non-presence, or, more so, its constant folding and unfolding into fields of possibility and non-possibility. It is not interconnectivity, but an *in-between*, anterior to the end of something and the beginning of something. It folds front-back-inward-down, as if one were looking down the horns of a mountain goat from the back of its <u>headless head</u>.

: : : : : : :

Originating at the point between
a laceration and the peak of a mountain.

: : : : : : :

Sitting here alone in thought as the summit of the negative.

: : : : : : :

The Stylinaut Triumvirate
(Mission Consultants):

the Cosmon(o)t
(the Outsider; the nay-sayer)

the Cosmo-nau(g)ht
(who stalls all at the temple of Nihill)

the Ambivert
(I and/(n)either Thou)

:::::::

Space treaties with secret species.

:::::::

Colossal Sanhedrin.

:::::::

Hopper of Mountain.—Climbing up the face of a sleeping grasshopper, the one that has implored this ascent. Its (mountain) face is rough, perceived as that akin to confluence of curvature-at-a-distance, but with the smoothness of onyx. He is colossal. I climb not (on) him but *through* him, wading into the immensity of his occult caves without entering them. He awakes—bids me welcome.

The reality of that plane is right Now, which is to say, *in* the grasshopper's face while also *on* it. And his antennae are our fingers, and are the width of the distance between us, which is the inverse of space, the enfolded density of the utterness of light. Relax, and kiss the unbearable heaviness of the non-experience. Simply unmask it and say, "Hello, Grasshopper. How are you?"

: : : : : : :

Funneled.—Non-perspectivism, in its folding and unfolding, recants a phrase—"to funnel." Like the trimming of a mane, one can cut off the ends of the system, severing a part in time. But the roots are always already feeding the system, severing the autonomy of its own death.

: : : : : : :

Adam Kadmon
Astonishing the
Amarok Wolf and
Admonishing the
Albatross

: : : : : : :

Juxtaposition.—At its limit, the Will wyrdly wills its own is-ness, juxtaposing a monism against a pluralist herd of impossibilities.

: : : : : : :

Time, Receptacle of the Cycle of Trauma.—A way to recognize the cycle of trauma is to pierce time—to reach the cycle's origin point. If you do not find the origin of the trauma, then you will forever be caught in the enactment of the cycle. One needs the trauma to move through the trauma. This is a cosmic law.

: : : : : : :

There are ghosts in here larger than your brain; crab apples falling as rain.

: : : : : : :

EYE cannot believe your I's.

: : : : : : :

To look away by seeing through.

To see, thoroughly looking.

: : : : : : :

Always seeing
what is not there,
sight coughed up,
seeing through
the liver of a saint.

: : : : : : :

Stricken naught.
Not stricken.
Strikingly knotted.

Knot strictures.

No structure.

Knot being.
Naught another being.
No other being.

: : : : : : :

Solar Wheel of the Year-long Sandstorm.

:::::::

Being not, unlike being, is as is not.

:::::::

Life has
nothing
to do
with you.

:::::::

(Keep falling into the ever-present crevasse of yourself and perhaps one day you will crawl out the other side and back into your True Self, emerging like the hero you always already were, but first had to kill to become!)

Pillar V: Stunner

| |
| |
| |
| |
| |
| |

([K]night of Cusps)

: : : : : : :

On bewildered cusps to bliss.

: : : : : : :

A furious sandstorm pumping caulk into androgynous fields of clay.

: : : : : : :

AUTOPHAGIC WORLD

: : : : : : :

All signs now read:

Do not betray the bewildering path to nowhere.

: : : : : : :

I fell in love with a simple piece of clay, just as Eve inversely fills the void of Adam's abyssic chest cavity.

: : : : : : :

My shadow slept with the Gatekeeper so that I could find God in the ordinary.

: : : : : : :

Tremors of the seven gates crawling up your spine,
lifting the shroud that houses this bad faith in yourself.

: : : : : : :

Ask not, yet ye be asked.
Think not, and none shall pass.

: : : : : : :

The pity they have for themselves.

: : : : : : :

Looming is the detritus.... the fates of lives lived incoherently.

:::::::

The games you cannot yet play.

:::::::

One cannot not worry until one has utterly worried completely.

:::::::

Hovering like ghosts among the saints.

:::::::

Shame is the sham which you caress,
tonguing the breasts of a life-lived-through-others.

The things they cannot not know.
Puppets—amorphous and unwise.

:::::::

Defer not to their will.

: : : : : : : :

Rumors: the words of crypto-lemmings masturbating in human skin, each stroking the magnetic polarity of their own horrific birth.

Crowds: the conjoined umbilical cords of a fleeting universal thought.

: : : : : : : :

Surnames: the purgatorial nomenclature of spectral hovering; folk spirits engrossed in the gross world.

: : : : : : : :

To know God is to incessantly love. To love is to incessantly know God without knowing oneself. To love others is to love God and love God alone.

: : : : : : : :

Asthmatic winds chime rottenly from the diseased opening of an overbearing mouth. If it is true that one hears not the winds but only the rustling of the leaves, then truly these respiratory winds have long since died.

: : : : : : :

Identity: a morsel for a crow.... a pickled pig's foot at a picnic for recovering lobotomy patients.

: : : : : : :

Loosing footing atop this perilous crevasse and falling out of myself.

The mind's eye holds a solitary view of nothing, connecting communally to everything.

: : : : : : :

A spasmodic well filled to the brim with a thousand darknesses....
each darkness carrying with it its own utter death.

: : : : : : :

Quietness: the tracheal tube that lovingly hoards the exponential remnant waves of Onan's last breath.

: : : : : : :

Diadems of the psychotropic stratosphere congregating around the whispers heard in ears: "Hell hath no fury like a mind unwound," they say, and the brain gallingly and gratefully tingles.

: : : : : : :

the world tears us apart,
leaving us in pieces

lick away the shadows

and may All drift along
in shorn shores of
sempiternal beneficence

: : : : : : :

There are stories told among wise men of an anarcho-mystical honeycomb of being, the cell-sphere wherein one licks oneself eternally at the foot of Mount Sinai. There is no politics there. There is only everything else that ever ought to be.

: : : : : : :

Monad nomad.

: : : : : : :

The recalcitrant muskeg of not being staggered by being.

: : : : : : :

To divorce oneself.

: : : : : : :

Penniless at
a gaffe station.
Giraffed, and
siphoning to
the nines.

: : : : : : :

Arctic fucks from wretched witches. Icing these shores… memories of their misses.

: : : : : : : :

There are kings in the water.
There is water in the witch.

: : : : : : : :

You are the weeping wind.

: : : : : : : :

beyond the seeping sin
its tentacles rescind

: : : : : : : :

Unruly and unbridled, this day has come to visit, as if the immanence of seven thousand derelictions is not ceaselessly housed within the contingent spontaneity of every single second.

: : : : : : : :

The Dead of Olde gathered around a fire to give talks to the brethren about the coming of age of humankind. "There will be so many of them that think they know, but they should attain knowledge of nothing," spoke a degenerate sage. He was hung by the elders. He is now known as a martyr among the Overmen of New. They hung him because they knew we should attain to not know. They hung him to make a martyr of him because they knew by not knowing. And for this, they will rise again in those who do not know.

:::::::

It seems like only yesterday (but it was not) that Fate was given the preponderance of a cloud.

To carefully tie the opposite of the knot that holds one's thoughts to one's mind.

:::::::

A bantering whale
warding off the imminent
beaching
of her calf.

: : : : : : : :

Heinous is the heresy of an unkempt whisper, of a mouth that contorts to a size smaller than the distance between the nostrils.

: : : : : : : :

A Voice speaking in the tongues of seven shamans is heard by no one at the center of the world. This Voice is the opposite of ontic castration: the permeating penumbra of all plausible apostasies.

: : : : : : : :

I do not know why one would really want to write about anything at all. But one ought to write incessantly anyways. Or not.

By the by, I do not want to have the thought of even having a thought about thinking about any of this.

: : : : : : : :

This entire sentence is putting on a clinic on self-deception.

Language: a petering realm of vertiginous chaos mocking my own ineptitude to fully know God.

: : : : : : :

Castration Complex.—Young men harnessing the strength of titans only to lose their footing on the grounds of misunderstanding a morality play.

: : : : : : :

A puzzled man with long limbs and a short torso walked down the hallway and up into the clouded view of his own symmetry.

: : : : : : :

The 'third heaven' as the un-projection of the Reality you are already in if you could only WAKE UP.

: : : : : : :

The cataclysmic expiations the dumbfounded give one another as they slosh themselves silly, bringing more and more and more numb souls into the *world-as-they-know-it.*

: : : : : : :

The furtive, virginal sweetness
of an ecstatic glance.

Like a sonic beatitude.

The taste of manna
consumed by a mountain goat.

: : : : : : :

Desire: more or less
of a flesh witch.

The resident hex
of your brain's
cosmic fissures.

: : : : : : :

The mute demiurge to become the opposite of alkaloid;

to remain at peace as the world's tongue rots within the outside of your mouth.

:::::::

The manicular reprisal of a rabbit's foot in my grave.

:::::::

Tapping into the inevitable and impossible tunnel-well which springs in and out of the cosmos.

:::::::

To circumscribe not the depth of one's actions according to the will's intention, but the depth of the will according to one's intention of non-action.

:::::::

Given of identities, life is terrible. Given terror, life is unlivable. Unlivable, life is horrible. Horrible, the impossible is possible. Plausible, even more of the possibly impossible.

:::::::

Fired in the boardroom of the All for fixating on ideas of "himself, oneself, he is, I…."

Opinions: bags of hair confusing the ontic and the ontological.

:::::::

To be but the malleability of melting periwinkles, simmering outside an inverted kettle hanging over a fire of oneself.

:::::::

Perhaps there is no closure. Perhaps there is just emptiness. Perhaps that festering wound just gets farther and farther away, which is to say, opens totally to infinity.

Pascal had his abyss. There is also the Immensity (that which eats the horizon) and the Elder (he who, off to the right, drips with age).

:::::::

Force fed Lemurian
canticles, rescinding
threats, and rebinding
sacred thread-bare
books, barring teeth at
time and whispering to
the point of having to
wait forever.

:::::::

There, the same oldness in the grimace, cataracted and unkind, thought full of baggage and scruff. While nowhere, the Everything, open, undiminished, thoughtlessness upon the unthought, opens Love divine.

:::::::

Flirtatious libations cast at one another through egotistical, mitigated glances.

Trusted fidelity to the tired, old hegemony of oneself, stalled individuation appears in your eyes, encroaches upon the universe as a hag.

: : : : : : : :

O, to walk
oneself
out
of the into.

: : : : : : : :

Glowing in the nonpit of Saturnine despair where all is devoured.... devours even despair, even devourment itself.

: : : : : : : :

The mouth of God has never closed, has no reason to eat anything other than everything.

: : : : : : : :

The reversal of this smile as the absence of my identification with it; where when I look into your eyes, I see complete unrelatedness, total freedom.

: : : : : : :

She dances, but with thoughts about dancing, and so has never danced a day. She never thinks about dancing, and so dances always, like a divine ballerina. Toes atop the floorless floor, beautifully indexical feet, pointing at dancing's dancing.

: : : : : : :

The illimitable realms of freedom available within you, which you will never access if you keep living like you know every goddamned thing.

: : : : : : :

no one to be
nowhere to go
nothing to do

: : : : : : :

The blood of time reflected
in the river's rays of glistening sand.

The mouth of a gentle
whisperer leading
herself into a thousand
winded breaths.

: : : : : : :

Saying nothing that might corrupt the pure, solitary gesture of your own "looking over there" right then.

Sitting alone with oneself in a room full of others. And to realize that one can be fully alone with oneself when no one is there.

: : : : : : :

NOW takes no sides.
There are no bygones on the other side of Now.
There is never no not not Now.

: : : : : : :

To escape confusion by being completely confused.

: : : : : : : :

Something so dry and raised about the fragment—
reading like the skinning of a goose pimple.

: : : : : : : :

Epigrammicide.

: : : : : : : :

N(e)rrative theory.

: : : : : : : :

Immensities of light streaming beyond everything everywhere, and yet there you remain: a piqued grey cube hidden behind the double curtain of is-ness.

: : : : : : : :

The correlation without causation of God's eternal non-correlational immersion in everything other than what I think I just thought about.

: : : : : : :

Emptying
embodying
unending.

: : : : : : :

The text as disembodied voice speaking from the abyss/
the abyss as disembodied text speaking from the voice.

: : : : : : :

Theory of the Savant-Garde.

: : : : : : :

Those who understand will understand. Those who know will know. Those who do not understand will not understand. Those who do not know will not know until they know.

: : : : : : :

The spiritual reconnaissance mission of diurnally finding oneself out as one's worst enemy.

: : : : : : :

Contrapuntal binocularity: listening to seeing as being's unending terra firmality.

: : : : : : :

Knowing that you also understand, through the inter-subjective auto-subversion of our co-mutual unknowing.

: : : : : : :

Sarcophagi theophany
Cacophony of harmony

: : : : : : :

Have you known of a world that never-knew fear? All is known and it knows that it begins Here.

: : : : : : :

Bodhi-pressure.

: : : : : : : :

A simple freak,
he walked among the meek
into perpetual bliss….

Pillar VII: Glower

(Walking Through Walls)

:::::::

I have swallowed the desert's winter flower.

:::::::

NOW calls as the corona of your glow.

:::::::

Reversed the revered,
cephalic indifference
eating on the brain, a lofty,
hearty sucking—on grain.
In this non-dream falls a
mighty stone, and out comes
a smile, the inversion of a
groan.

:::::::

Floating like plummeting is falling as raining.

: : : : : : :

Landfills of wood sharpening as spinning;
boats of silver hogs whispering as blooming.

Tiny pearls aging as aching;
holy tolls sinking like striving.

: : : : : : :

gaseous peaks
pining as swirling;
restored is the Bay,
the river as churning

heaving, and then
holy hearths,
ten new hearts and an
earthworm

: : : : : : :

blotted hot clouds of dust
played in the style of Wagner,
aligning and misshapen,

a tone once mistaken as
passing laughter

pounds of gray hay
sitting as bucolic,
in the charnel ground
Mesmer calls; -ized and
unbridled

:::::::

A woman at the edge of the block fell into a crack that ran all the way through to the center of the earth. After walking twelve hundred miles, she had stumps for legs. Three hours later, she was glided back to the city and said that there were angels hovering above the catacombs of the saints. Bodhisattva of the blemished ones, she walks through walls.

:::::::

Spinningly—dancing and hop-like.

: : : : : : :

Skipping over oneself
and strumming
a reflecting golden harp.

A cold winter balancing
on the tip
of a warm plate.

Light without light
within light.

: : : : : : :

Somnambulant and awakened.

Being nowhere
and having nothing
to say about it.

: : : : : : :

Tender and the nebulousness.

Forthrightly daringly.

: : : : : : : :

There are many ways,
but there is only the Way.

: : : : : : : :

Eyes mell thought.

: : : : : : : :

A gleaming bulb attaining at the apex
of the inside of your eyes.

An unsight seen through
unsoughtly insights:

insightly unsought non-thoughts.

: : : : : : : :

Sleeping like a giant in the candelabra's fur.

: : : : : : :

Eyes are blood melons,
sweet and staunch,
laughing, unclogged,
and floating with nymphs.

: : : : : : :

Hearing one's reflection in the mirror.

: : : : : : :

The non-scape of sound's bolded druthers, a voice, my own, piercing the echoed, hollow grandeur of being's shallowing waters—a whispered sentience glowing in my pupils.

: : : : : : :

the winds of chime,
timeless, and
erodingly—

of this breath,
and its thousands of whispers
this it points at me

:::::::

Automata(do[Or]).—All of a sudden, in the middle of a compartment with no doors, no windows, not even a floor. Magnanimous bliss gyrating in the abyss! Who will save the bull that runs into us always?

:::::::

Joys of tears—
uplifting the supplanted.

:::::::

Very especially this second—
never don't not forget.

:::::::

Suddenly, ex nihilo, and a darting cherub...

: : : : : : :

Freefalling out of Life
watching it as if from a hill
with no ground.

: : : : : : :

The desire without object-ing to not c(r)aving under pressure.

: : : : : : :

Feasting off the familiar.

: : : : : : :

Rainbowery ploys.

: : : : : : :

Hyper-vibrant auto-floriography.

: : : : : : : :

A fire blooming on a fig tree.
Starting a flower underneath you.

: : : : : : : :

jumping into the grave
and out of grave concern

Out jumping the gravely concerned.

gravitating from the leaven
and levitating on the grave

: : : : : : : :

multiversal Womyn
playing the strings of
re-instrumenstruation

Wingedly strident,
flung, and flying.

: : : : : : : :

An inverted inner laughter sets the world at bay. Yet even the world standing still cannot touch the thrill that is on its way.

: : : : : : : :

Stereographic predilections.

: : : : : : : :

Unrepetitive dyadlectics.

: : : : : : : :

Trigo(g)nomic gumptions.

: : : : : : : :

There was a beautiful light that used to cast its shadow upon the glimmering nose of an old king. Each morning, he picked cherries from his favorite tree. It is said that the king had no fear of anything in the land, and that the cherry tree told him the secrets of how to run his kingdom. For forty-two years the king picked cherries, until one day he walked outside to see the tree had been hit by lightning and all the cherries were gone. He called in three people to assess the damage: the knight, the jester, and the village idiot. The knight took his sword and offered to cut down the tree. The king stopped him and said there was no need. The jester tried to make light of the situation by offering to make a pie filled with nothing but emptiness. The king kindly dismissed the jester and did not chuckle. Finally, the village idiot walked up to the tree. He thanked the tree for what it has offered the king, serving him all those years without ever asking anything for itself. Upon hearing the idiot's words, the king ordered the knight to take the idiot to the kitchen for a feast. He had not eaten in almost three days, for he and his family were poor. When they arrived in the kitchen, the king found four large dishes overflowing with cherries. It is said that underneath the earth lies the secret seeds of life. One only needs to bury oneself deep enough to never find them. Only then will one know the true meaning of the idiot's revelation—that the idiot was a sage who had long eaten of the jester's pie.

: : : : : : : :

Never-loafing around nowhere.

Always-running about everywhere.

:: :: : : : :

Jestering towards apt gestures.

: : :: : : ::

Stones thrown a-way.

:: : :: : : :

Hemlock,
and the
Asklepieion doorway.

: : :: : :: :

I have fallen apart, and away,
the Way,
always and all ways.

I am lead back in through the ancient doorway,
which was never closed or open,
always there,
and never there.

: : : : : : :

Indivisibly invisible.

: : : : : : :

The funereal site of oneself as the living conundrum of divine fire. Flaming and immutable, this is the glowing body of All-amorphous splendors, and we walk among the dead as the Now-alive.

: : : : : : :

Breathing—
never short of breath—
and glowing—
always glowing—
never short on breathing.

: : : : : : :

UNDERNEATH, AND
SEEING THE SOUNDS
OF ANGELS' WINGS.

: : : : : : :

Love permeates all things. You've merely been deflecting it with yourself!

: : : : : : :

This is unlike anything, that is, nothing.

: : : : : : :

EATING MEMORY.

: : : : : : :

The world is the gulf that floats us away;
liquidity,
and a bulbous moon
points (at) the Way.

: : : : : : :

Like a copper queen
Like little waves of light
We sing, we sing
We do not cannot fight

: : : : : : :

Rhythmic, this loss is continual.

: : : : : : :

I walk out into the darkness that shines within the space outside of the inside of my cosmic opposite, that thing-that-is-not-me—*but IS truly*—when I turn off my thinking of it. When the plains meet the foot of the hill and the ground turns sideways up into the air—only when I side-walk the tilting crevice of being does the earth come up to meet me, and at that in between space, where space is no longer space but just a vanquished thought, is where I exit myself, enter into not myself in between where I do not walk on the earth and where I stopped thinking of it.

: : : : : : : :

And that is where the end begins.
And that begins the end of where.
And so, ends the beginning of me.
And so, begins the end of my thinking it.

: : : : : : : :

For, I cannot think side walking the tilting crevice of being, but just walk—under myself and over the river's edge, into the nonplace, the nothing other than walking in between the tilted valley of heaven, the tilted valley of never-not-knowing anything other than not not knowing the complete and utter in between of the out-of, the placeless place that is none other than, is always, the Ur-center of the hollowed-out earth, where molten lava flows into its own inverted gorge, and all that has ever been is no more, and is forever, right on the tip of the tongue of the first thing I ever whispered to myself |in secret|, and the very last breathe I just took before I remembered that I was breathing.

: : : : : : :

On the edge of the valley in between the hill of a thousand steps and the one thousand thousandths sits the dirge for something other than the anything that once was, and Here, nowhere, does this space reveal utter, complete Marvel.

: : : : : : :

Acu(ity)puncture.

: : : : : : :

circularity rising,
walking, musing,
eating, shining; and
drones hoping
for lords to come

: : : : : : :

Sheen shifting.

: : : : : : :

Unloosing salamanders.

Loosening the loss.

Groves of grooves,
if any, and always.

: : : : : : :

my dreams were opals,
shine-shivering
through immortal
fields of pneumatic bliss

: : : : : : :

Epi(ec)static.

: : : : : : :

The love-f(l)ur(r)y of a thousand suns auto-germinating abreast the st(a)rnum and the pollinating of the pleasures of the sol-ar plexus.

: : : : : : :

The Flower Man of the Indigo Gate.

: : : : : : :

Wearing a sky that grew taller.

: : : : : : :

Anarcho-optimistic perfectionism.

: : : : : : :

hover-genuflection—floatante religiosio

: : : : : : :

Seeing with the clarity of a thousand suns scorching
with the clarity of seeing.

: : : : : : :

Quantum Crypto-Poetry

: : : : : : : :

Swallowing mercenaries.

: : : : : : : :

The All grows our heads in fire.

: : : : : : : :

Having tasted God.

Epilogue: Pedagogigs Of The Saturnine (Onwards, Jonah, To Nineveh!)

"Melancholy redeems this universe, and yet it is melancholy that separates us from it."

—E. M. Cioran

...True dat.

—Saturn

The story goes that one day, Sophia, the aforementioned philosophy student of the great Dr. Hemlock, and later an acolyte of Fremont the Stylite, returned home to the West after meditating at the foot of Pillar Five for nine months and took a walk in the forest near her home in the Northeastern countryside. It is said by locals that this forest was once inhabited by Eastern Woodlands tribes, indigenous Native Americans who migrated South from the region of Canada several hundred years ago. The trees in this area were said to tell stories of antecedent cosmic events. Hawks circle the sky, catalyzing the synergy between above and below. After eventually making her way to a particular clearing atop the hill, Sophia stopped to do some pranayama breathing underneath the enveloping branches of an evergreen tree. Withdrawn, she was overcome with a deep sadness over her existence. And via that feeling, in that state of being, she felt the presence of an uncanny figure. Deep in thought, she calmly whispered, "Hello, old friend." Saturn had come to visit.

Though this most recent encounter transpired under an aegis of tranquility, it is a stark contrast to the first time, which, at one point, nearly scared her out of her mind. Sitting in her room late one night, the hair stood up on the back of her neck as she perceived from a vantage within herself a spectral figure across the room that was staring straight through her like a bullet moves through Jell-O. A year or two later, for a variety of reasons, she started therapy with a woman who specialized in cognitive neuropsychiatry. When she brought it up to the neuropsychiatrist, she said that it was a likely a form of sleep paralysis, perhaps what is known as a hypnagogic hallucination. To Sophia's then-mind, the term hypnagogic hallucination was a cop-out. "Yea, okay, I get it," she thought, "but WHY?"—Did she even hear what he was telling her? *She was awake.* Talk about invalidating!

Over the years, though, she began to integrate dark recesses like those into her being, and what she eventually learned, through a kind of mystico-traumatic gnosis, is that all that dark, eerie stuff became fodder for a spiritual and ethical life. And so, the figure of Saturn developed into a kind of friend or welcome guest.

: : : : : : :

Saturn is quite a paradoxical cat. Cascading along Heraclitan Rivers, the waters of which rise from the shedding of its own panpsychic tears, he mourns over himself perpetually, simply because he cannot do otherwise. He is a placeholder to the liminal state between being and non-being, ensuring its double erasure in the physical plane. Lacking the potential for self-knowledge that is afforded to human beings, Saturn's blessings are at once its plight.

Long considered an archetypal figure by scholars and initiates alike, accounts of Saturn vacillate among several historical contexts and necessitate the perplexities of individuation. In Saturn some see a demon, whereas others see a luminous figure. In folklore, he is the Beast who, upon falling in love with Beauty, turns into a striking prince. In astrology, Saturn holds the qualities of a malefic planet. Theosophists call such a being the Guardian at the Threshold. Jungian psychology would attribute to Saturn the features of the shadow. Neuropsychiatry distinguishes it as phenomena effectuated by a hypnagogic hallucination. Whether one wishes to see in him all or none of these traits, one thing is for certain: Saturn, a figure blanketed in melancholy, is well-equipped to teach us about pain and suffering.

Broadly speaking, melancholy can be understood as form of existential sadness. Sigmund Freud, for instance, in his 1917 essay "Mourning and Melancholia," regarded it as a stifling of the mourning process, an arrested moment in a mourner's life which disables and immobilizes their identification with the dead, the shadow, or the past self over which they mourn. But this is just one definition of melancholy. In quite a different way, medieval mystics, such as John of the Cross or the Author of the *Cloud of Unknowing*, would have identified sadness as an essential element of their spiritual lives. Taking this route, one can understand Saturn as an etheric evocation of a sacred melancholy, one that simultaneously deepens and negates a longing for the absolute. Saturn substantiates the penchant for spectral images, fissures in language, and time/space hybridities that inheres within mourning. But it is also that which brings Sophia closer to the divine.

:::::::

When she returned home after her walk in the forest, Sophia began to think about what had just happened and wrote down the following in her notebook:

> The reversal: Saturn evokes a pure love, leading me into myself at the very horizon of myself, beyond the territory of the knowable. Saturn came to thee, for he knew nowhere else to go. Why, one might ask, would he deviate from the non-knowledge of himself? Everything is holy. Once cast from the formless fear that led him here, he was begotten of himself, bred in the oncogenic cellar of masochistic desire. You now pet him at the center point betwixt the brows wherein self-discipline meets self-knowledge, thus feasting at the table where he once sat, watching you from within you.

> Fear is but the black landscape of the Watcher, the one who led you astray in the vastness of yourself, confining you to a monadic cell.
>
> ...Fear not suffering. The body must awaken.

A quizzical logic can be said to permeate these words, as they attempt to describe a realm as shadowy as the language used to describe it. Yet perhaps the underlying influence of this logic is not to solve anything, but rather to lie something bare—to show that there is a puzzle there at all. And in that way, it makes a kind of logical sense. "Suffering, teaching and transformation. What is necessary," Simone Weil once wrote, "is not that the initiated should learn something, but that a transformation should come about in them which makes them capable of receiving the teaching."[11] When she was younger, Saturn took on the shape of her inner most fears. Her sufferings became atonements for the karmas of her past lives. Now, Saturn, the ethereal imprint of dark matter, urges her to keep going, to tread into the unknown, to become whatever it *is* that she is.

---

11 *Gravity and Grace.* Trans. Emma Crawford and Mario von der Ruhr. London and New York: 2002, 83.

The last line from her notes can also to be read as a kōan of sorts, a playful but concentrated gesture of language that gives pause. On the one hand, to 'fear not suffering' is to accept the spiritual concept rendered in the Pali word *dukkha*, which is, as Buddhist doctrine teaches, the first noble truth: life is suffering. On the other hand, that 'the body must awaken' implies a double logic: for the body to awaken, one must not fear suffering, and this suggests that the body remains, at least allegorically speaking, in a state of slumber. Or, put another way, the body is inhabited by a sleeper and, as such, so Frank Herbert's saying goes, the sleeper—in this case, the one with a body—must awaken. Thus, to *have* such fearlessness of suffering, the body must *already be awake.*

In that case, Saturn could be thought to divulge certain esoteric truths at work that relate specifically to the alchemy of the body. Medieval alchemists might have seen in Saturn the necessity of what they call nigredo, or the blackening phase of the alchemical process, and in the body a vessel. Works of spiritual alchemy such as *The Book of Lambsprinck* and *Aurelia Occulta Philosophorum*, for instance, make few references to physical alchemical processes, but illustrate inner processes of nigredo, likening this blackness to the head of a raven.[12] Keeping in mind that the real goal of alchemy was psycho-spiritual transmutation, one can think of this melancholy over the body as a conduit to a kind of acephalic repose.

: :: : : : :

Sophia soon recalled a conversation she had with some friends when she was young. It was one of those conversations that, interspersed with jests and housed within the perpetuity of youth, felt so mundane at the time, but that now she could not imagine her life without. Somehow, they got to talking about what it might be like if one were blind. The resounding answer seemed to be that one would see black. But she had to disagree. If one were,

---

12 Cf. "I am an infirm and weak old man, surnamed the dragon; therefore am I shut up in a cave, that I may become ransomed by the kingly crown ... A fiery sword inflicts great torments on me; death makes weak my flesh and bones ... My soul and my spirit depart; a terrible poison, I am likened to the black raven, for that is the wages of sin; in dust and earth I lie, that out of Three may come One. O soul and spirit leave me not, that I may see again the light of day, and the hero of peace whom the whole world shall behold may arise from me" (Zadith bin Hamuel, *Aurelia Occulta Philosophorum*, in Jean-Jacques Manget [Johann-Jacob Mangetus] (ed.), *Bibliotheca Chemica Curiosa* 2, 1702:198-212).

let's say, blind since birth, they wouldn't have a clue what the color black looked like. So, they stood there, like ravens mulling over obsidian seeds. Then, out of nowhere, one of her friends remarked, "It's like… what do you see out of your ears? *Nothing*." Smartest thing she had ever heard.

Fire is only as hot as it is burning. A hole is only as deep as it is dug. *Saturn is only as visible as he is nothingness*. As the great yogis and mystics might say, the body is an impermanent dwelling place for a number of spiritual faculties that can be developed in a human being. It follows, then, that if you are unfortunate enough to experience lots of pain and suffering, then you are fortunate enough to have opened vast spaces of nothingness within your own body. This nothingness becomes essential to a spiritual practice.

:::::::::

Looking back on it, that she met Saturn again, this time on a walk in the forest, is not so much a daunting realization as it is a Dantean one. "When I had journeyed half of our life's way, / I found myself within a shadowed forest, / for I had lost the path that does not stray," writes

Dante Alighieri in the opening lines of the *Inferno*.[13] When she was younger her soul entered into the dark forest and was thus charged with walking through the Nine Circles. This time around, Saturn afforded her a moment for anamnesis, for self-remembrance: she must continue on the path to Paradise.

In all its darkness and density, Saturn illuminates the hidden possibilities of sadness. Saturn's pedagogy of melancholy encourages us to darkly suffer in the light of self-knowledge, to nurture a love in which sadness becomes sacred, a non-suffering of absolute, radical freedom. Wrapped in sovereignty, the whole vicinity of the body is overcome by an ecstatic joy: *that* the body suffers compels the matter of what it suffers over: we are HERE, which is really *nowhere*, the non-vessel of everywhere. The saturnine, in all its initial unintelligibility and paradox, thus recuperates the ultimate condition of *satori*—of fearing not suffering in an awakened body—and compels the infinite potentiality of Love.

---

13 *Inferno.* Trans. Allen Mandelbaum. New York: Alfred A Knopf, 1995, 59.

∞

Ø

∞

Ø

∞

Ø

∞

Ø

∞

Ø

∞

Ø

∞

Ø

∞

Ø

∞

Ø

∞

Ø

∞

~

~L

~La

~La

~La f

~La fi

~La fi

~La fin

~La fin

~La fin e

~La fin es

~La fin est

~La fin est

~La fin est l

~La fin est le

~La fin est le

~La fin est le c

~La fin est le co

~La fin est le com

~La fin est le comm

~La fin est le comme

~La fin est le commenc

~La fin est le commence

~La fin est le commencem

~La fin est le commenceme

~La fin est le commencemen
~La fin est le commencement
~La fin est le commencement~

Brad Baumgartner is the author of several works, including *Stylinaut* (Spuyten Duyvil), *The–Tempered Mid·riff: A Play in Four Parts* (Schism - Neuronics), *Celeste: Our Lady of Flowering Marvel* (Spuyten Duyvil), *Quantum Mechantics: Memoirs of a Quark* (The Operating System), and a monograph entitled *Weird Mysticism: Philosophical Horror and the Mystical Text* (Lehigh University Press). He currently teaches English at Penn State University.

www.ingramcontent.com/pod-product-compliance
Lightning Source LLC
Chambersburg PA
CBHW011150190726
48288CB00010B/3261

* 9 7 8 1 9 5 6 0 0 5 0 0 4 *